David Skinner

The Cloud of Unknowing

AND

The Book of Privy Counseling

The Cloud of Unknowing

AND

The Book of Privy Counseling

Edited and with an Introduction by
William Johnston

Foreword by Huston Smith

IMAGE BOOKS
DOUBLEDAY
New York   London   Toronto   Sydney   Auckland

An Image Book
PUBLISHED BY DOUBLEDAY
a division of Bantam Doubleday Dell Publishing Group, Inc.
1540 Broadway, New York, New York 10036

IMAGE, DOUBLEDAY, and the portrayal of a deer
drinking from a stream are trademarks of Doubleday,
a division of Bantam Doubleday Dell Publishing Group, Inc.

First Image Books edition published September 1973.

Library of Congress Catalog Card Number 73-79737

ISBN 0-385-03097-5

35 37 39 40 38 36 34

For
Dan McCoy

ACKNOWLEDGMENTS

I wish to express my deep gratitude to the Reno Carmelites without whose kind help this edition could not have been made. In particular I would like to thank Laureen Grady for her painstaking work on the Middle English text and Elizabeth Reid for her beautiful typing. To the whole community I am grateful.

The Cloud of Unknowing

AND

The Book of Privy Counseling

FOREWORD
Huston Smith

William Johnston's Introduction to this book places it in its historical setting so admirably that it frees me to make the only two additional points that I think might help the reader get into it. First, is there something about these final, countdown years of our millennium that justifies a new edition of this mystical text? And second, with all the commentary that has already been lavished on the key word in its title, "unknowing," is there still something to be said about it?

On the first score, new winds of the spirit seem to be blowing today, the chief reason being that we no longer feel caged by science. Science itself never did cage us, but we built ourselves a cage from its reports, which we then unwittingly entered. Hearing from science only news of the physical universe, we jumped (illogically) to the conclusion that matter is all that exists—or if not quite all, then at least the bottom line.

Quantum mechanics has changed that. From immaterial wave packets from which particles derive, to space whose ten original dimensions collapsed at the beginning of time to form the tiny superstrings of which subatomic particles consist, quantum mechanics is telling us that the universe of space, time, and matter derives from something that exceeds those matrices. Science doesn't go on to add what the author of the book in hand would have added—that the transcendental object is Spirit—for science cannot deal with such things. But for those who have ears to hear, that possibility is there. It is as if seventeenth-to-nineteenth-century materialism was a tremendous storm that the jetliner *Modernity* has had to climb through to reach cruising altitude. We still haven't quite reached that altitude, for cultural lag is a strong headwind. But brilliant patches of sunlight are breaking through —frequently enough to remind us that the weather reports from traffic control towers include one we haven't heard for a long time: "Atmosphere clear, vision unlimited."

If those thoughts are suggested by the word "cloud," what about the word "unknowing"?

If it were synonymous with ignorance it would not be interesting, but it takes only a page or two for us to realize that the author of this book is using the word in a vastly more portentous sense. For the ignorance that he is occupied with—"obsessed with" would not be too strong—is of a distinctive kind; it is the kind of which mysteries are constituted. Problems have solutions, but mysteries don't, because the more we understand a mystery the more we realize how much more there is to it than we had realized at the start. The larger the island of knowledge, the longer the shoreline of wonder.

Implicated with mystery, the cloud of unknowing will never disappear, but it can to some distance be penetrated. How? By activating a faculty of knowing that parts the obscuring clouds of words and thoughts. The underlying idea here is the limitations of language, and no topic has received more philosophical attention in the last half-century; Heidegger, Wittgenstein, and Derrida have all wrestled with it. But (to borrow a Buddhist figure of speech) though they see that language is only a finger pointing at the moon and not the moon itself, *The Cloud* surpasses them in attending more helpfully to the pointing finger. This is an important service, for on nights when the sky is overcast, it is important to know where to look for the moon if one hopes to catch glimpses of it through fleeting rifts in the coulds. Technically speaking, *The Cloud* uses *kataphasis* (what can be said) to face us in the direction where the moon hangs, and this positions us to take *apophatic* (unsayable) advantage of openings that appear.

4

Unless the *via negativa* works with a solid *via positiva* to extend its trajectory, we are left looking around aimlessly and emptily.

How are we to penetrate the language barrier?

To pierce any obdurate object, say a block of ice, we need a pick with a sharp point and a heavy mallet to propel it. To obtain its sharp point, *The Cloud* advises compressing oceans of words, first into short phrases, and then (by further compression) into single syllables, the first of which is "sin" and the second "God." These are anything but nonsense syllables. They are mantras that distilled generations of understanding down to single vocables. The word "sin" encapsulates the entire Christian understanding of our separation from God, and "God" connotes what we have been separated from and are returning to.

As for the mallet that empowers the mantra, it is love, life's strongest force. But we should be clear. The love our author makes central to his method is more than an emotion. It is an informed emotion which responds to the object that attracts it. We do not know the full nature of that object, veiled as it is by the cloud we are seeking to penetrate. But we do know that *if* we knew it in its fullness we would find it more wonderful than words can describe and images depict.

Having said that, all I want to do is get out of the way as fast as I can and leave the reader with an author who understands these things far better than I do.

INTRODUCTION

Recent times have witnessed a revival of interest in Western mysticism. It is as though the West, long exposed to Zen and Yoga and the spiritual systems of the East, now searches for its own tradition and its own spiritual heritage. Strangely enough, the interest in mysticism is not just academic. It is also practical. Many people are anxious to read the mystics in order to practice the doctrine they teach and to experience the states of consciousness they depict. In short, interest in Christian mysticism is part of a widespread craving for meditation, for contemplation, for depth—a desire to get beyond the changing phenomena and the future shock and the global village into a deeper reality that lies at the center of things. Mysticism is no longer irrelevant; it is in the air we breathe.

In such a climate, those in search of a mystical guide could do no better than turn to the anonymous fourteenth-century author of *The Cloud of Unknowing*. Here is an Englishman, at once a mystic, a theologian, and a director of souls, who stands in the full stream of the Western spiritual tradition. A writer of great power and of considerable literary talent, he has composed four original treatises and three translations; and in this book his two principal works, *The Cloud of Unknowing* and *The Book of Privy Counseling*, are rendered into modern English from the original texts. I believe that the reader who surrenders himself to the author's mystical charm will find in their very perusal a truly contemplative experience.

The two books complement each other. *The Cloud* is well known as a literary work of great beauty in its style as in its message. Widely read in the fourteenth century when

7

it was written, it has never lost its honored place among the spiritual classics of the English language. *The Book of Privy Counseling*, on the other hand, is less famous. It is the work of the author's maturity; and, as so often happens, the older writer has lost some of the buoyant charm of youth. This makes his later work more difficult reading; but any loss of charm is more than compensated for by a theological precision, a spiritual depth, and a balanced authority that have come with years of profound experience. Now he is self-confident, convinced beyond all doubt that, whatever anyone may say to the contrary, the contemplation he teaches is of the highest value. This later book is in many ways a book of counseling as we understand this word today. It is the work of a man who is friendly, anxious to give help and counsel—a man endowed with keen psychological insight, who knows the human mind, who is aware of man's tragic capacity for self-deception and yet is endowed with a delicate compassion for those who suffer as they struggle to remain in silent love at the core of their being. But his counseling, it must be confessed, is not the non-directive type about which we today hear so much. Rather is it authoritative—the guidance of a man who has trodden the mystical path himself and offers a helping hand to those who will hearken to his words. If this edition now offered to the public has any unique value, it may be because of the inclusion of *The Book of Privy Counseling*.

Practical Guide to Contemplation

The two treatises, then, are eminently practical. They guide the reader in the path of contemplation. While there is an abundance of books teaching meditation of the discursive kind, not so many teach the contemplative prayer that goes beyond thought and imagery into the supraconceptual cloud of unknowing. And it is precisely this that the English author is teaching. In his rejection of conceptualiza-

8

tion he is as radical as any Zen Buddhist. All thoughts, all concepts, all images must be buried beneath a cloud of forgetting, while our naked love (naked because divested of thought) must rise upward toward God hidden in the cloud of unknowing. With the cloud of unknowing above, between me and my God, and the cloud of forgetting below, between me and all creatures, I find myself in the *silentium mysticum* about which the English author read in the work of Dionysius.

If *The Cloud* is radical in its rejection of conceptualization, even more so is *Privy Counseling*, the opening paragraph of which contains words that set the theme for the whole treatise: "Reject all thoughts, be they good or be they evil." This is pretty stark. God can be loved but he cannot be thought. He can be grasped by love but never by concepts. So less thinking and more loving.

The meditation that goes beyond thought is popular in the modern world, and it is for this reason that I find these two books particularly relevant today. As for the way of getting beyond thought, the English author has a definite methodology. After speaking of good and pious meditations on the life and death of Christ, he introduces his disciple to a way that may well be attractive also to the modern reader, namely the *mantra* or sacred word:

If you want to gather all your desire into one simple word that the mind can retain, choose a short word rather than a long one. A one-syllable word such as "God" or "love" is best. But choose one that is meaningful to you. Then fix it in your mind so that it will remain there come what may. This word will be your defense in conflict and in peace. Use it to beat upon the cloud of darkness above you and subdue all distractions consigning them to the cloud of forgetting beneath you. Should some thought go on annoying you, demanding to know what you are doing, answer with this one word alone. If your mind begins to intellectualize over the meaning and connotations of this little word, remind yourself that its value lies in its simplicity. Do this and I assure you these thoughts will vanish. Why? Because you have refused to develop them with arguing. (p. 56)

As can be seen, the little word is used in order to sweep all images and thoughts from the mind, leaving it free to love with the blind stirring that stretches out toward God.

In *Privy Counseling* the author speaks of two clear-cut steps on the way to enlightenment. The first is the rejection of all thoughts about *what* I am and *what* God is in order to be conscious only *that* I am and *that* God is. This is what I would like to call existential prayer because of its abandonment of all essences or modes of being. But it is only the first step. The second step is the rejection of all thought and feeling of my own being to be conscious only of the being of God. In this way the author leads to a total self-forgetfulness, a seemingly total loss of self for a consciousness only of the being of him whom we love. This is interesting doctrine. How can we twentieth-century men who talk so much about personality accept it?

The Loss of Self

Let me first say that this problem of the loss of self is extremely relevant in the religious climate of today, a climate that is largely dominated by the meeting of the great religions in a common forum and a fascinating dialogue that historian, Arnold Toynbee, has not hesitated to call the most significant event of the century. In this East-West religious encounter and exchange, the central problem on which all discussion finally focuses is that of the existence and nature of the self. Can a highly personalized religion like Christianity find common ground with an apparently self-annihilating system like Buddhism? This is a problem that has constantly come to the fore in ecumenical meetings I myself have attended. Anyone confronted with it would do well to listen to the wisdom of this English author. Steeped in the Christian tradition, he speaks a language that Buddhists understand. He is indeed a great spokesman for the West.

Let us consider some of the passages in which he justifies his advice to forget one's own being.

In *The Cloud* he claims that to feel one's own existence is the greatest suffering possible to man:

> Every man has plenty of cause for sorrow but he alone understands the deep universal reason for sorrow who experiences that he is. Every other motive pales beside this one. He alone feels authentic sorrow who realizes not only *what he is*, but *that he is*. Anyone who has not felt this should really weep, for he has never experienced real sorrow. (p. 103)

This is a remarkable passage. It might seem like a rejection of life and of existence, were it not for the author's explicit statement that this is not his meaning:

> And yet in all this, never does he desire to not-be, for this is the devil's madness and blasphemy against God. In fact, he rejoices that he is and from the fullness of a grateful heart he gives thanks to God for the gift and the goodness of his existence. At the same time, he desires unceasingly to be freed from the knowing and feeling of his being. (p. 104)

It is clear that the author is not advocating self-annihilation; nor is he denying the ontological existence of the self. Rather is he saying that there is an awareness of self that brings joy and gratitude; and there is awareness of self that brings agony. What awareness of self causes this great sorrow?

It seems to me that Christian mysticism can be understood only in the light of the resurrection, just as Buddhist mysticism can be understood only in the light of nirvana. Until the resurrection, man's personality, his true self, is incomplete. This holds even for Christ, of whom Paul says that "he was constituted Son of God by a glorious act in that he rose from the dead" (Rom. 1:4). In other words it was

11

through the resurrection that Christ was perfected, finding his true self and ultimate identity. Until this final stage, man is inevitably *separated* from his end. And not only man but the whole universe, which is groaning in expectation for the sons of God to be revealed.

This imperfect state of incompleteness, isolation and separation from the goal is the basic source of man's existential anguish—anguish that arises not because of *his existence* but because of *his separated existence*. Sorrow for this separation, says the author, is much more fundamental and much more conducive to humility than sorrow for one's sins or anything else. Hence the anguish running through the writings of the mystics and reflected in the agonized cry of a St. John of the Cross: "Whither hast thou hidden thyself, O my beloved, and left me to my sighing?" Here the mystic is separated from the beloved whom he has inchoately experienced; and he longs for completion, for union, for the goal. If this means death, joyfully will he die—"Break the web of this sweet encounter." As if he were to say, take away the veil that *separates* me from my beloved and my all. Clearly the anguish is that of separation and incompleteness at the level of existence. One can experience one's incompleteness emotionally or economically or culturally or sexually; and all this is painful. But how terrible to experience it at the deepest level of all, that of existence! For all these other sorrows are partial experiences of one root experience of existential contingency. And this, I believe, is the sorrow of the man who knows not only *what he is* but *that he is*.

All this is not far removed from the anguish of the existentialist philosophers about which we at one time heard so much. Their agony was not necessarily theistic. Rather did it come from a radical sense of man's insufficiency, contingency, incompleteness, mortality, summed up in Heidegger's terrible definition of man as "being-to-death." Here again it is not precisely existence that causes the trouble, but limited existence. Man, faced with the prospect of extinction, is not in control of his own destiny.

12

So much for the existentialists. With the English author it is mainly in *Privy Counseling* that the notion of *separation* with all its suffering is stressed. But now his language is more precise. The suffering of man is not *that he is* but *that he is as he is;* and the author makes his existential prayer: "That which I am and the way that I am . . . I offer it all to you." (p. 156) Now he has made it abundantly clear that the problem is not existence itself but limited existence, and so he has no need for further explanation.

At the beginning of his treatise he makes a statement that echoes through the whole work: "He is your being and in him you are what you are." Lest this sound pantheistic, the author quickly adds, "He is your being, but you are not his," as if to remind us that while God is our being we are not God. But having made this distinction he keeps stressing that the great suffering and illusion of man is his failure to experience that God is his being. Rather does he experience his being apart from God. The whole aim of his direction is to lead us to the experience that "he is your being and in him you are what you are." It is not in isolation, not in separation from the totality that man finds his true self; but only in God. The knowledge and feeling of any self other than this must be destroyed.

This leads to the inexorable law that the incomplete self must die in order that the true self may rise. "Unless the grain of wheat falling into the ground dies, itself alone remains; but if it dies it brings forth much fruit."

In this context we can perhaps understand the author's relentless assertion that the thought and feeling of self must be annihilated. Yet this annihilation is less terrible because it is the work of love: "For this is the way of all real love. The lover will utterly and completely despoil himself of everything, even his very self, because of the one he loves. He cannot bear to be clothed in anything save the thought of his beloved. And this is not a passing fancy. No, he desires always and forever to remain unclothed in full and final self-forgetting." (p. 172) If we love, death will inevitably

13

follow and self will be forgotten with terrible finality. But it will be a joyous death. Let me say a word about the connection between love and death.

In the Thomistic philosophy to which the English author is so faithful, love is "ecstatic" in that it takes us out of ourselves to live in the thing we love. If we love money, we live in money; if we love our friends, we live in them; if we love them in God, we live in God. This means that in love there is a real death, as St. John of the Cross (again a thoroughgoing Thomist) expresses in his enigmatic words: "O life, how canst thou endure since thou livest not where thou livest?" Is this because his life, no longer in his body, is palpitating in the one he loves? And he wonders how this life can continue. For death is an inevitable consequence of ecstatic love.

The dilemma is terrible. If man refuses to love, his separated self remains in its agonized isolation without ultimate fulfillment, even though ontologically God is in his being. If he loves, he chooses death for the separated self and life for the resurrected self. And it is the resurrected self that is at work in contemplation, which will never cease. "For in eternity there will be no need for the works of mercy as there is now. People will not hunger or thirst or die of the cold or be sick, homeless and captive. No one will need Christian burial for no one will die. In heaven it will no longer be fitting to mourn for our sins or for Christ's Passion. So, then, if grace is calling you to choose the third part, choose it with Mary." (p. 76)

This brings us to the question of the relationship of the true self to the all. The author writes that there is a total union ("He is your being") and yet it is not total because I am not God's being ("You are not his"). A strict Thomist of the fourteenth century, he would probably have explained this according to the Platonic notion of ideas in the mind of God—that creation exists from eternity in his mind, so that there is a total unity side by side with variety. To experience this would be "chaste and perfect love" in which one is

14

united with God "blindly"; that is to say, without thoughts or feelings or images of any kind, experiencing oneself in God and through God. St. John of the Cross seems to be getting at this when he says that at first we experience the Creator through his creatures, but at the summit we experience creatures through the Creator.

Yet I myself believe that this metaphysic is less meaningful to modern man than the dynamic approach of Teilhard de Chardin. This is more biblical, giving centrality to the risen Christ Omega as well as to the resurrection of all men. It sees the ultimate eschatological union as a total indwelling of God in man and man in God and all in Christ going to the Father in accordance with the words of Jesus in John 17. As for the paradox that all is one and not one, Teilhard answers with a principle that runs through all his work: in the realm of personality, union differentiates. When I am most united with God, I am most myself. Here union is clearly distinguished from annihilating absorption: it is in union with the other that I find my true self. Incredible paradox? Yet we explain the Trinity in some such way. And does not the principle that union differentiates apply also to human unions and interpersonal relationships? In the deepest and most loving union with another, far from losing ourselves we discover our deepest selves at the core of our being. If this is true of human relationships, it must also apply to the most intimate union of all: that of Yahweh with his people.

I have attempted to explain the author's position on the loss of self, which is an integral part of his direction and a relevant problem in the modern religious scene. But I must quickly confess that the author is reluctant to offer explanations and probably does so only as a concession to the learned divines who may read and criticize his book. How often he remarks that "only he who experiences it will really understand." If there is a problem, it exists only at the verbal or metaphysical level, while at the level of experiential love it is simply a non-problem since then one knows existentially

15

what it is to lose self and find self at the same time. The whole endeavor of the author is not to explain (for no explanation is possible) but to lead the disciple to a state of consciousness where he will see it for himself. "And so I urge you: go after experience rather than knowledge. On account of pride, knowledge may often deceive you, but this gentle, loving affection will not deceive you. Knowledge tends to breed conceit, but love builds. Knowledge is full of labor, but love, full of rest." (p. 188) This is like the Zen Buddhists, who without explanation, insist that you must simply *sit* in meditation.

The Place of Christ

Another point that is crucial in these two books as in the works of all the Christian mystics concerns the place of Christ. Briefly the problem is this: Christian theology, following the New Testament, situates Christ at the very heart of prayer—Christ the man, the Incarnate Word. But how does Christ the man fit into this imageless, supraconceptual void? Where is Christ when I am between the cloud of unknowing and the cloud of forgetting? This is quite a dilemma; yet I believe that the author of *The Cloud* can truly be called Christocentric.

Let me say first that we can consider Christ in his historical existence or in his risen existence. In either case it is, of course, the same Jesus; but the mode of existence is quite different. About the historical Christ we can have thoughts and ideas and images, just as we can picture the villages through which he walked; but of the risen Christ we can have no adequate picture. This is stated categorically by St. Paul who, when asked what the resurrected body looks like, retorts (if I may translate him into modern jargon), Don't ask stupid questions! "But someone will ask, 'How are the dead raised? With what kind of body do they come?' You foolish man! . . . For not all flesh is alike, but there is one kind for men, another for animals, another for birds, and another for fish." (I Cor. 15:35–38) So there are many ways of existence and the resurrected way is different from that we now enjoy.

Now the Christian, following St. Paul, does not pray just to a historical figure but to the now existing risen Christ who contains in himself all the experience of his historical existence in a transformed way, as he indicated by showing his wounds to his disciples. As for the way of talking about the Christ who lives in our midst today, Teilhard de Chardin, influenced by the later Pauline epistles, speaks of "the cosmic Christ" who is co-extensive with the universe. By death the body is universalized, entering into a new dimension and into a new relationship with matter. It is in this dimension that the risen Christ is present to us. This is a dimension that we too enter by death; but in life also we can somehow touch it by love in the cloud of unknowing.

The English author is, I believe, speaking about the cosmic Christ, though he does not have this terminology. In fact he makes a brilliantly orthodox union of the historical and the risen Jesus in the Mary Magdalene motif, which obviously appeals greatly to him:

In the gospel of St. Luke we read that our Lord came to Martha's house and while she set about at once to prepare his meal, her sister Mary did nothing but sit at his feet. She was so intent upon listening to him that she paid no attention to what Martha was doing. Now certainly Martha's chores were holy and important . . . But Mary was unconcerned about them. Neither did she notice our Lord's human bearing; the beauty of his mortal body or the sweetness of his human voice and conversation, although this would have been a holier and better work . . . But she forgot all this and was totally absorbed in the highest wisdom of God concealed in the obscurity of his humanity.

Mary turned to Jesus with all the love of her heart, unmoved by what she saw or heard spoken and done about her. She sat there in perfect stillness with her heart's secret, joyous love intent upon that *cloud of unknowing* between

17

her and her God. For as I have said before, there never has been and there never will be a creature so pure or so deeply immersed in the loving contemplation of God who does not approach him in this life through that lofty and marvelous *cloud of unknowing*. And it was to this very cloud that Mary directed the hidden yearning of her loving heart. (p. 71)

From the above it is very clear that entering the cloud does not mean abandoning Christ. Jesus is present: he is the divine center to which Mary's love is directed. But she has no regard for clear-cut images of his beautiful mortal body, no ears for the sweetness of his human voice. She has gone beyond all this to a deeper knowledge, a deeper love and a deeper beauty. Here in practice is the paradox of a contemplation that is at once Christocentric and imageless.

Examples of this imageless approach to the man Christ abound in the English author; nor is it necessary here to quote his reference in *Privy Counseling* to Christ who is at once the porter and the door. Or his interesting interpretation of the ascension of Christ, who has to go ("It is expedient for you that I go") lest the disciples become so attached to his historical body that they cannot love his glorified body. As I have said, our word "cosmic" is not there; but the idea is inescapably present.

With the realization that Christ is co-extensive with the universe, a whole cosmic and social dimension enters into contemplation. Christian mysticism can never be selfish preoccupation with one's little ego; it must be an opening to other people and to the universe. Once again, the English author explains this in the cosmology of his day.

For when you fix your love on him, forgetting all else, the saints and angels rejoice and hasten to assist you in every way—though the devils will rage and ceaselessly conspire to thwart you. Your fellow men are marvelously enriched by this work of yours, even if you may not fully understand how; the souls in purgatory are touched, for their suffering is eased by the effects of this work; and, of course, your own spirit is purified and strengthened by this contemplative work more than by all others put together. (pp. 89–90)

No corner of the universe is untouched by this exercise of love. Put in Teilhardian terms we might say that the noosphere is built up by this contemplative exercise; or that fresh impulse is given to the thrust of consciousness in its movement toward Omega. It is, of course, a great paradox that we should help people precisely by forgetting them: "Therefore, firmly reject all clear ideas however pious or delightful. For I tell you this, one loving blind desire for God alone is . . . more helpful to your friends, both living and dead, than anything else you could do." (p. 60) This is something known only to experience through faith.

The increasingly cosmic and social dimension of contemplation is stressed in *Privy Counseling* where this work is described as a development from "bodiliness" to "ghostliness"; and I have translated these words as the Pauline "flesh" and "spirit." For Paul, of course, flesh is not the sensual, Platonic flesh; it is not the instinctual part of man. Rather does it mean man rooted in this world; and when Paul uses it in a pejorative sense, it means man seeing only this world and blind to anything beyond it. On the other hand, the spiritual man is the man open to the universe and under the influence of the Spirit. Hence growth in contemplation, a growth toward spirit, is a development toward cosmic consciousness so that the contemplative puts on the mind of the cosmic Christ and offers himself to the Father for the salvation of the human race. Here, indeed, is the very climax of the author's thought, couched in the beautiful prayer of *Privy Counseling*:

> That which I am and the way that I am,
> with all my gifts of nature and grace,
> you have given to me, O Lord, and you are
> all this. I offer it all to you, principally
> to praise you and to help my fellow Christians
> and myself. (p. 156)

This is truly the peak-point when the contemplative together with Christ offers himself to the Father for the human race. Now he has put on the mind of Christ so completely that, in a sense, only the Father remains. It is Christ within who prays and offers himself to the Father—"I live, now not I, but Christ liveth in me." And, of course, the whole prayer is eminently Trinitarian and bafflingly paradoxical. There is one God, who is my very existence. And yet my existence is somehow distinct and I can offer it to him.

In this Christology, however, some readers may be perturbed by the author's use of the Bible. Here, as in *Privy Counseling* and throughout his works, his apparent twisting of Scripture to illustrate and prove his point may bring a smile to the lips of the modern exegete. Yet this approach is typical of the mystics from Origen to John of the Cross. And it is, I believe, legitimate, and even helpful to the modern exegete.

That there is a distinctively contemplative approach to Scripture was indicated by Vatican II when it wrote: "For there is a growth in the understanding of the realities and the words handed down. This happens through the contemplation and study made by believers who treasure these things in their hearts through the intimate understanding of spiritual things they experience." (*Document on Divine Revelation*, Chapter 2, 8) Growth in understanding comes from the mystics who, so to speak, live the Scriptures from within. If it is true, as Paul says, that no one can understand the spirit of a man except his own spirit, how true, too, that no one can really understand the Scriptures (however much his exegesis) except he who possesses the Spirit that composed them. The contemplative approach to Scripture complements the exegetical and is, I believe, coming more and more to the fore today.

Primacy of Love

From what has been said it will be clear that in the English author the central place in the contemplative exercise is allotted to love. That love is the essence of the whole thing is unequivocally stated again and again in words like the following:

> For in real charity one loves God for himself alone above every created thing and he loves his fellow man because it is God's law. In the contemplative work God is loved above every creature purely and simply for his sake. Indeed, the very heart of this work is nothing else but a naked intent toward God for his own sake. (p. 80)

So the very heart of this work is love, which the English author refers to as a "secret little love," a "naked intent of the will," a "blind outstretching," a "gentle stirring of love," "this work," or simply as "it." It should be noted, however, that he uses these expressions for an activity that *includes* knowledge or consciousness of some kind. For purposes of analysis it is possible to speak of knowledge and love in contemplation; but the activity the author speaks of is a blend of both, a completely simple experience arising in the depth of the contemplative's heart: in the last analysis it is indescribable, as the author declares when he says that "Whatever we may say of it is not it, but only about it." (p. 169) He has no doubt, however, that its predominant element is love and it is upon this that he puts all the emphasis. The practice of unknowing with its treading down of all distinct knowledge beneath the cloud of forgetting is no more than preparation for the cultivation of this blind stirring that is the most important thing in life. This is reiterated many times, as, for example, in such words as the following:

> And so to stand firmly and avoid pitfalls, keep to the path you are on. Let your longing relentlessly beat upon the *cloud of unknowing* that lies between you and your God. Pierce that cloud with the keen shaft of your love, spurn the thought of anything less than God, and do not give up this work for anything. For the contemplative work of love by itself will eventually heal you of all the roots of sin. (p. 63)

This, a typical passage, shows how the business of forgetting is relegated to a secondary place, being no more than a means of making room for the "keen shaft of . . . love," which, however, is accompanied by a deep consciousness of God. Instances could be multiplied where the author waxes enthusiastic about the little love that comes to dominate in the mystical life. "Your whole personality will be transformed, your countenance will radiate an inner beauty, and for as long as you feel it nothing will sadden you. A thousand miles would you run to speak with another whom you knew really felt it, and yet when you got there, find yourself speechless." (pp. 182, 183) As the contemplative enters more deeply into the cloud, love comes to guide him, teaching him to choose God, who cannot be thought or understood or found by any rational activity. As it grows stronger, it comes to take possession of him in such a way that it dominates every action. It orders him to choose God, and if he does not follow its command it wounds him and gives him no peace until he does its bidding. This is beautifully illustrated in a passage from another work of the author which does not, unfortunately, appear in this book. Let me quote from *An Epistle of Stirrings* about the dynamic quality of the blind stirring of love:

Then that same that thou feelest shall well know how to tell thee when thou shalt speak and when thou shalt be still. And it shall govern thee discreetly in all thy living without any error, and teach thee mystically how thou shalt begin and cease in all such doings of nature with a great and sovereign discretion. For if thou mayest by grace keep it in custom and in continual working, then if it be needful to thee for to speak, for to eat in the common way, or for to bide in company, or for to do any such other thing that belongeth to the common true custom of Christian men and of nature, it shall first stir thee softly to speak or to do that other common thing of nature whatso it be; and then, if thou do it not, it shall smite as sore as a prick on thine heart and pain thee full sore, and let thee have no peace but if thou do it. And in the same manner, if thou be speaking or in any such other work that is common to the course of nature, if it be needful and speedful to thee to be still and to set thee to the contrary, as is fasting to eating, being alone to company, and all such other, the which be works of singular holiness, it will stir thee to them.

From the above it can be seen that the blind stirring of love eventually develops into a bright flame, guiding the contemplative's every choice. It stirs him softly and sweetly to act; but it also impels him to do God's will with a certain inevitability against which it is useless to struggle: he seems to be in the grip of something more powerful than himself that he must obey at the risk of losing interior peace when it smites upon his heart. That this is the guidance of God himself is indicated in *The Cloud* where the author speaks of the guiding action of God in the very depths of the soul to which no evil spirit can penetrate and on which no reasoning can make impact. And this, I maintain, is the very apex of Christian morality. No longer fidelity to law but submission to the guidance of love.

Moreover it is precisely this love that gives wisdom, the truest knowledge. Indeed the meditational process taught by the English author could be described in three stages. First there is the clear and distinct knowledge brought by discursive meditation. This is abandoned for the guidance of love. Then this love finds wisdom. In yet another work, *A Treatise of the Study of Wisdom,* the author describes this process with a traditional simile. As a burning candle enlightens both itself and the objects around, so the light of love enables us to see both our own wretchedness and the great goodness of God:

As when the candle burneth, thou mayest see the candle itself by the light thereof, and the other things also; right so when thy soul burneth in the love of God, that is when thou feelest continuously thine heart desire after the love of God, then by the light of his grace which he sendeth in thy reason, thou mayest see thine unworthiness, and his great goodness. And therefore . . . proffer thy candle to the fire. (S.W. 43:8)

A similar doctrine is taught by Aquinas, who holds that a great love of God calls down the Spirit, according to the promise of Christ at the Last Supper that if anyone loved him he would be loved by the Father, who would send another Paraclete: progress in charity, then, means progress in wisdom. This kind of wisdom is, I believe, apparent in human relations where love can discover beauty and potentiality that reason alone cannot find.

And so the author stands in the stream of tradition that regards mysticism as a love affair between the bridegroom and the bride, between Yahweh and his people. It is here that the deepest significance of Western mysticism is to be found.

Dionysius

This Englishman belongs to a tradition known as "apophatic" because of its tendency to emphasize that God is best known by negation: we can know more about what God is *not* than what he is. Influenced by Neoplatonism, it is a doctrine that owes much to Gregory of Nyssa and Dionysius the Areopagite. To this latter the author of *The Cloud* acknowledges his debt at the end of his book: "Anyone who reads Denis' book will find confirmed there all that I have been trying to teach in this book from start to finish." (p. 139) That these words are sincere is proved by the fact that the English author made a translation of Dionysius' *Mystical Theology*, which goes by the name of *Hid Divinity*. Yet recent scholars have pointed out that he was less Dionysian than he himself supposed. One reason for this is that no medieval could get an objective view of the writings of the Areopagite. Only comparatively recently was it established with certainty that Dionysius was a Syrian monk of the early sixth century; for the medievals he was St. Paul's convert writing to Timothy with an authority close to that of the Scriptures themselves. His writings had influenced not only the Greek mystics, notably Maximus the Confessor in the eighth century, but also after the translation of John Scotus Erigena in 877 they made an incalculable impact on the whole Latin Church. Commentaries were multiplied; Albert, Aquinas and Bonaventure received Dionysian influence; even Dante sang the praises of the Areopagite. Consequently, the Dionysius who came to the author of *The Cloud*, like the Aristotle who sometimes comes to modern Thomists, was overlaid with a tradition that no medieval would have recognized. And it was this embellished Dionysius that influenced the English author. Moreover, he makes no secret of the fact that he will not follow the "naked letter" of Dionysius' book; he intends to interpret it himself and to make use of other interpreters. He almost certainly did not read the original text of Dionysius but used the Latin translation of Joannes Sarracenus together with the commentary of Thomas Gallus, Abbot of Vercelli.

Yet, granted that Dionysius has been somewhat embellished in the years that elapsed between the sixth century and the fourteenth, it still remains true that his basic ideas are fundamental to the thought of the author of *The Cloud*. I shall, therefore, first briefly set forth his doctrine.

According to Dionysius, there are two ways in which man can know God: one is the way of reason (λόγος); the other is the way of mystical contemplation (μυστικὸν θέαμα). Rational knowledge of God is obtained through speculative theology and philosophy; but mystical knowledge is greatly superior to this, giving a knowledge of God that is intuitive and ineffable. Hence, it is called "mystical" or "hidden." Dionysius speaks much of the transcendence of God, stressing the fact that by reasoning we know little about him; but he never denies the power of discursive reason to give some knowledge of God, merely emphasizing the superiority of mystical knowledge.

In fact, he teaches two ways of knowing God by reason—one affirmative and the other negative. We can affirm of God all the good that can be affirmed of his creation, saying that he is holy, wise, benevolent, that he is light and life. All these things come from God, so we can affirm that the source possesses their perfections in a higher way. But (and this is the point stressed by Dionysius) there is also a negative way of knowing God, since he is above all his creatures. He is wise, but with a wisdom different from that of men; his beauty, goodness, and truth are different from those we know. So, in a sense, God is unlike anything we know: we must keep in mind that the ideas we have of him are totally inadequate to contain him.

But there is yet a higher way of knowing God. "Besides the knowledge of God obtained by processes of philosophical and theological speculation, there is that most divine knowledge of God which takes place through ignorance"; in this knowledge the intellect is illuminated by "the insearchable depth of wisdom." Such knowledge is not found in books nor can it be obtained by human effort, for it is a divine gift. Man, however, can prepare himself to receive it; and this he does by prayer and purification. Here is Dionysius' advice:

Do thou, then, in the intent practice of mystic contemplation, leave behind the senses and the operations of the intellect, and all things that the senses or the intellect can perceive, and all things which are not and things which are, and strain upwards in unknowing, as far as may be, towards the union with Him Who is above all things and knowledge. For by unceasing and absolute withdrawal from thyself and all things in purity, abandoning all and set free from all, thou shalt be borne up to the ray of divine darkness that surpasseth all being.

(*De myst. theol.*, I, 1)

The point of Dionysius is that since the human senses and intellect are incapable of attaining to God, they must be "emptied" of creatures or purified in order that God may pour his light into them. In this sense they are in complete darkness in regard to created things but they are at the same time filled with light from God. Hence, we can say that "The Divine Darkness is the unapproachable light in which God is said to dwell." When the faculties are emptied of all human knowledge there reigns in the soul a "mystic silence" leading it to the climax that is union with God and the vision of him as he is in himself.

Such is the doctrine that flows through the apophatic mystics to the time of St. John of the Cross. The fundamental point is that our ordinary faculties, sensible and intellectual, are incapable by themselves of representing God to us; that is why their ordinary use must be abandoned. God is above anything we can picture in our imagination or conceive in our mind. The fourth and fifth chapters of Dionysius' *Mystical Theology* give a formidable and detailed catalogue of the things God is *not* like. First of all, no sensible thing resembles God, so that "we remove from him all bodily things, and all these things that pertain to body, or to bodily things—as is shape, form, quality, quantity, weight, position, visibility, sensibility . . . For he is neither any of these things nor hath any of these, or any or all these sensible things." Again, he is like nothing we can conceive in our mind—and once again there follows the remarkable catalogue of the spiritual things that God is not like. Such is the negative theology that underlies apophatic mystics.

In his translation of the *Mystica Theologia* the English author makes some additions to the original text. Chief among these is his insertion of love as the most important element in contemplative prayer. In this he advances on Dionysius and probably follows an earlier writer, Thomas Gallus, whose commentary he must have used. I have already spoken at length about the English author's emphasis on love but let me quote one more passage in *The Cloud* where we find a Dionysian stress on the inadequacy of knowledge joined to a new and powerful stress on the centrality of love:

Try to understand this point. Rational creatures such as men and angels possess two principal faculties, a knowing power and a loving power. No one can fully comprehend the uncreated God with his knowledge; but each one, in a different way, can grasp him fully through love. Truly this is the unending miracle of love: that one loving person, through his love, can embrace God, whose being fills and transcends the entire creation. And this marvelous work of love goes on forever, for he whom we love is eternal. (p. 50)

In this way the English author, starting from a Neoplatonic framework, has entered more and more deeply into a contemplation that is filled with Christian love. In some ways, indeed, his whole work can be considered as a hymn to love like that of the great Spaniard who sang, "O living flame of love, that tenderly wounds my soul in its deepest center!"

Throughout this introductory essay I have stressed the author's doctrine of love not only because it is the key to all his thinking but also because it is particularly relevant for our day, when science is exploring "altered states of consciousness" that are not unlike the states toward which the mystic points. No need to speak here of biofeedback, mind control, drugs, and other techniques for leading people beyond thought to the silent, intuitive consciousness. What distinguishes the contemplation taught by the English author and the other Christian mystics is the centrality of love. Motivated by love, it is a response to a call which issues in mutual *agape* —and any change of consciousness is no more than a consequence of this naked intent of love.

Historical Background

By now my reader is surely anxious to learn more about this author. But unfortunately external evidence is minimal and little can be said. No doubt the best way to know him is by reading his works, where, if anywhere, the style is the man. No one has succeeded in putting a name on him, though many attempts have been made; nor do we know to what religious order he belonged, if indeed he was a religious. So successful was his humble desire to remain anonymous. Manuscripts of his works, however, are rather numerous, the oldest dating back to the beginning of the fifteenth century. Since the author seems to have known the work of Richard Rolle and since Walter Hilton seems to have known *him*, historians conclude that he wrote in the late fourteenth century. This is corroborated by his style, which, moreover, indicates that the treatises were written in the northeast Midlands.

He belongs to a century made famous in the annals of spirituality by the names of Richard Rolle, Juliana of Norwich, and Walter Hilton in England; by Meister Eckhart, John Tauler, and Henry Suso in Germany; by Jan van Ruysbroeck in Flanders; by Jacopone da Todi and Catherine of Siena in Italy. This is an age associated with the names of Angela de Foligno and Thomas à Kempis. It is an age when, in spite of troubles and rumbling presages of a coming storm, Europe was deeply religious: faith penetrated to the very hearts of the people and influenced not only their art, music, and literature, but every aspect of their lives. Merry England was saturated with a religious faith that breaks forth in *Piers Plowman* and the *Canterbury Tales*. Chaucer may laugh goodhumoredly at the foibles of nuns and friars, but he accepted the established religion with an unquestioning mind. Such was the society in which the author of *The Cloud* lived and wrote: both he and his public took for granted a Church, a faith, and a sacramental life that are no longer accepted without question by many of his readers today.

He was, then, a thoroughgoing medieval, steeped in the spirit of his time and imbued with its tradition. So many of his words, phrases, and ideas are also found in *The Imitation of Christ*, in the *De Adhaerendo Deo*, in the writings of the Rhineland mystics, and in the other devotional treatises of the time that one immediately sees him as part of a great current of medieval spirituality. He was aware, too, of what was being said and thought throughout Christendom, for there was no splendid isolation at that time; English monks and scholars were frequenting the great centers of learning throughout Europe.

If proof were needed of his traditionalist character, one has but to mention his constant reference not only to the Scriptures but also to Augustine, Dionysius, Gregory, Bernard, Aquinas, Richard of St. Victor, and the rest. Modesty and fear of vanity forbid him from quoting these authors at length, but he cannot escape referring to their works and reflecting their thought. And again, the wealth of tradition underlying his writings breaks through in the figures and illustrations that fill his pages. The "cloud of unknowing" itself, the Martha-Mary motif, the picture of Moses ascending the mountain, the notion of the soul as a mirror in which one can see God, the comparison of mystical prayer to sleep, the "naked intent of the will," the "chaste and perfect love of God," "the sovereign point of the spirit"—all these are pregnant with tradition, used by so many Christian authors that it is well-nigh impossible to state categorically from whom the English author is borrowing or from whom he chiefly draws his inspiration.

But when one comes to study this author in his historical setting, there arises another point that here deserves mention; namely, his striking similarity to St. John of the Cross. Quite a few commentators have adverted to this, the English author being spoken of as a St. John of the Cross two centuries before his time. For it is true that almost every detail of his doctrine is paralleled in the later Spanish mystic—and not only the doctrine but even the words and phrases are in many cases identical. How account for this remarkable affinity?

It is not impossible that the Spanish mystic read the Latin translation of *The Cloud* which may have been circulating on the European continent of his day. However this may be, it seems clear that both writers belong to the same spiritual tradition. Through their pages speak Augustine, Dionysius, the Victorines, Tauler, Ruysbroeck, and the rest; and we know, moreover, that both were unrelenting Thomists. So it is the great stream of a common tradition that has formed the minds of these two men, both being part of a mystical current that has flowed through Christian culture, breaking down the barriers of space and time separating fourteenth-century England and sixteenth-century Spain; nor have its surging waves lost their power in the twentieth century.

In the notes I have given a list of cross references to the works of St. John of the Cross. These are not meant to be exhaustive but I think they are sufficient to show that both writers belong to the same tradition and perhaps they will help refute the theory, sometimes advanced, that the English author was a rebel, an outsider to tradition, a suspect and heterodox innovator. Nothing could be further from the truth. He is a most representative Western mystic, a reliable guide in the twentieth as in the fourteenth century; and his counsel will be of great value both to those who follow traditional prayer and to those who practice transcendental mediation or the other contemplative forms recently introduced from the East.

This Edition

Finally let me say a word about this edition, which is an effort to make the author's thought available and intelligible to the modern reader, particularly to the modern reader who would like to practice the kind of prayer that is here described. I have used as a basis the very excellent critical text of Professor Phyllis Hodgson: "The Cloud of Unknowing" and "The Book of Privy Counseling," edited from the manuscripts with introduction, notes and glossary, Oxford University Press, 1944 (reprinted 1958). Only once have I departed from this text. This is at the end of The Book of Privy Counseling. My last paragraph is not found in Professor Hodgson's edition. It is found, however, in some late manuscripts and I have included it in my edition simply because I feel that without it the book ends rather abruptly.

For Scripture quotations I have used the Douay version where the author's exegesis seemed to demand it. Otherwise I have used more up-to-date translations.

The title *The Book of Privy Counseling* I have retained as it is, partly because I feel that it is better not to tamper with the title of a classic and partly because it is more or less untranslatable. Besides, the word "counseling," as I have already pointed out, is meaningful for the people of our day. As for the word "privy," it implies both that the letter is not for everyone but only for those who will understand, and also that the contents are intimate and confidential. I think that both of these meanings are best retained by preserving the original word.

The chapter divisions in *The Book of Privy Counseling* are my own. The original text is all of a piece and has no chapters. I thought, however, that this edition would be more readable if the text were divided more or less in the same way as *The Cloud*.

Let me then conclude my part by making my own the words of the author: "My dear friend, I bid you farewell now with God's blessing and mine. May God give you and all who love him true peace, wise counsel, and his own interior joy in the fullness of grace. Amen."

WILLIAM JOHNSTON

Sophia University, Tokyo
September 1973

32

A Book on Contemplation
called
THE CLOUD OF UNKNOWING

which is about that cloud within
which one is united to God

CONTENTS

THE CLOUD OF UNKNOWING

Chapter

35

37

THE BOOK OF PRIVY COUNSELING

PRAYER

O God unto whom all hearts lie open
unto whom desire is eloquent
and from whom no secret thing is hidden;
purify the thoughts of my heart
by the outpouring of your Spirit
that I may love you with a perfect love
and praise you as you deserve.   Amen.

FOREWORD

In the name of the Father and of the Son and of the Holy
Spirit.

Whoever you are possessing this book, know that I charge
you with a serious responsibility, to which I attach the
sternest sanctions that the bonds of love can bear. It does
not matter whether this book belongs to you, whether you
are keeping it for someone else, whether you are taking it to
someone, or borrowing it; you are not to read it, write or
speak of it, nor allow another to do so, unless you really believe that he is a person deeply committed to follow Christ
perfectly. I have in mind a person who, over and above the
good works of the active life, has resolved to follow Christ
(as far as is humanly possible with God's grace) into the
inmost depths of contemplation. Do your best to determine
if he is one who has first been faithful for some time to the
demands of the active life, for otherwise he will not be prepared to fathom the contents of this book.

Moreover, I charge you with love's authority, if you do
give this book to someone else, warn them (as I warn you)

to take the time to read it thoroughly. For it is very possible that certain chapters do not stand by themselves but require the explanation given in other chapters to complete their meaning. I fear lest a person read only some parts and quickly fall into error. To avoid a blunder like this, I beg you and anyone else reading this book, for love's sake, to do as I ask.

As for worldly gossips, flatterers, the scrupulous, talebearers, busybodies, and the hypercritical, I would just as soon they never laid eyes on this book. I had no intention of writing for them and prefer that they do not meddle with it. This applies, also, to the merely curious, educated or not. They may be good people by the standards of the active life, but this book is not suited to their needs.

However, there are some presently engaged in the active life who are being prepared by grace to grasp the message of this book. I am thinking of those who feel the mysterious action of the Spirit in their inmost being stirring them to love. I do not say that they continually feel this stirring, as experienced contemplatives do, but now and again they taste something of contemplative love in the very core of their being. Should such folk read this book, I believe they will be greatly encouraged and reassured.[1]

I have divided this work into seventy-five chapters. The last one deals more specifically with the signs which indicate whether or not a person is being called to contemplative prayer.

INTRODUCTION

My dear friend in God, I beg you, stay alert and attentive to the way you are progressing in your vocation. And give thanks to God for this calling, so that with the help of his grace you may stand firm against all the subtle assaults of enemies who will harass you from within and without and so that you may come to win the reward of life unending. Amen.

CHAPTER 1

Of the four degrees of the Christian life; of the development of his vocation for whom this book was written.

My dear friend in God, I would like to pass on to you what I have roughly observed about the Christian life. Generally, it seems to progress through four ascending phases of growth, which I call the *Common*, the *Special*, the *Singular*, and the *Perfect*. The first three may, indeed, be begun and completed in this mortal life, but the fourth, though begun here, shall go on without ending into the joy of eternity. Do you see that I have arranged these stages in a definite sequence? This is because I believe that our Lord in his great mercy is calling you to advance by these steps. I discern his call to you in the desire for him that burns in your heart.

You know yourself that at one time you were caught up in the *Common* manner of the Christian life in a day-to-day mundane existence along with your friends. But I think that the eternal love of God, which had once created you out of nothing and then redeemed you from Adam's curse through the sacrifice of his blood,[1] could not bear to let you go on living so common a life far from him. And so, with exquisite kindness, he awakened desire within you, and binding it fast with the leash of love's longing, drew you closer to himself into what I have called the more *Special* manner of living. He called you to be his friend and, in the company of his friends, you learned to live the interior life more perfectly than was possible in the common way.

Is there more? Yes, for from the beginning I think God's love for you was so great that his heart could not rest satisfied with this. What did he do? Do you not see how gently and how kindly he has drawn you on to the third way of life, the *Singular*? Yes, you live now at the deep solitary core of your being, learning to direct your loving desire toward the highest and final manner of living which I have called *Perfect*.[2]

CHAPTER 2

A short exhortation to humility and to the work of contemplation.

Take courage, now, and frail mortal though you are, try to understand yourself. Do you think you are someone special, or that you have deserved the Lord's favor? How can your poor heart be so leaden and spiritless that it is not continually aroused by the attraction of the Lord's love and the sound of his voice? Your enemy will suggest that you rest on your laurels. But be on your guard against this treachery of his. Do not be deceived into thinking that you are a holier or better person because of your great calling or because you have progressed to the *Singular* way of life. On the contrary,

46

you will be a most pathetic and culpable wretch unless, with God's grace and proper guidance, you do all in your power to live up to your calling. Far from being conceited, you ought to be all the more humble and devoted to your heavenly Lord when you consider that he, the Almighty God, the King of kings and Lord of lords, has stooped so low as to call you. For out of all his flock he has lovingly chosen you to be one of his special friends. He has led you to sweet meadows and nourished you with his love, strengthening you to press on so as to take possession of your heritage in his kingdom.

I urge you, then, pursue your course relentlessly. Attend to tomorrow and let yesterday be. Never mind what you have gained so far. Instead reach out to what lies ahead. If you do this you will remain in the truth. For now, if you wish to keep growing you must nourish in your heart the lively longing for God. Though this loving desire is certainly God's gift, it is up to you to nurture it. But mark this. God is a jealous lover. He is at work in your spirit and will tolerate no meddlers.[1] The only other one he needs is you. And all he asks of you is that you fix your love on him and let him alone. Close the doors and windows of your spirit against the onslaught of pests and foes and prayerfully seek his strength; for if you do so, he will keep you safe from them.[2] Press on then. I want to see how you fare. Our Lord is always ready. He awaits only your co-operation.

"But," you ask, "how am I to go on; what am I to do next?"

47

How the work of contemplation shall be done; of its excellence over all other works.

This is what you are to do: lift your heart up to the Lord, with a gentle stirring of love desiring him for his own sake and not for his gifts. Center all your attention and desire on him and let this be the sole concern of your mind and heart. Do all in your power to forget everything else, keeping your thoughts and desires free from involvement with any of God's creatures or their affairs whether in general or in particular. Perhaps this will seem like an irresponsible attitude, but I tell you, let them all be; pay no attention to them.

What I am describing here is the contemplative work of the spirit. It is this which gives God the greatest delight. For when you fix your love on him, forgetting all else, the saints and angels rejoice and hasten to assist you in every way—though the devils will rage and ceaselessly conspire to thwart you. Your fellow men are marvelously enriched by this work of yours, even if you may not fully understand how; the souls in purgatory are touched, for their suffering is eased by the effects of this work; and, of course, your own spirit is purified and strengthened by this contemplative work more than by all others put together.[1] Yet for all this, when God's grace arouses you to enthusiasm, it becomes the lightest sort of work there is and one most willingly done. Without his grace, however, it is very difficult and almost, I should say, quite beyond you.

And so diligently persevere until you feel joy in it. For in the beginning it is usual to feel nothing but a kind of darkness about your mind, or as it were, a *cloud of unknowing*. You will seem to know nothing and to feel nothing except a naked intent toward God in the depths of your being. Try as you might, this darkness and this cloud will remain between you and your God.[2] You will feel frustrated, for your mind will be unable to grasp him, and your heart will not relish the delight of his love. But learn to be at home in this darkness. Return to it as often as you can, letting your spirit cry out to him whom you love. For if, in this life, you hope to feel and see God as he is in himself it must be within this darkness and this cloud.[3] But if you strive to fix your love on him forgetting all else, which is the work of contemplation I have urged you to begin, I am confident that God in his goodness will bring you to a deep experience of himself.[4]

CHAPTER 4

Of the simplicity of contemplation; that it may not be acquired through knowledge or imagination.

I have described a little of what is involved in the contemplative work but now I shall discuss it further, insofar as I understand it, so that you may proceed securely and without misconceptions.

This work is not time-consuming even though some people believe otherwise. Actually it is the shortest you can imagine; as brief as an atom,[1] which, as the philosophers say, is the smallest division of time. The atom is a moment so short and integral that the mind can scarcely conceive it. Nevertheless it is vastly important, for of this minute measure of time it is written: "You will be held responsible for all the time given you." This is entirely just because your principal spiritual faculty, the will, needs only this brief fraction of a moment to move toward the object of its desire.

If you were now restored by grace to the integrity man possessed before sin you would be complete master of these im-

49

pulses. None would ever go astray, but would fly to the one sole good, the goal of all desire, God himself. For God created us in his image and likeness, making us like himself, and in the Incarnation he emptied himself of his divinity becoming a man like us. It is God, and he alone, who can fully satisfy the hunger and longing of our spirit which transformed by his redeeming grace is enabled to embrace him by love. He whom neither men nor angels can grasp by knowledge can be embraced by love. For the intellect of both men and angels is too small to comprehend God as he is in himself.[2]

Try to understand this point. Rational creatures such as men and angels possess two principal faculties, a knowing power and a loving power. No one can fully comprehend the uncreated God with his knowledge;[3] but each one, in a different way,[4] can grasp him fully through love. Truly this is the unending miracle of love: that one loving person, through his love, can embrace God, whose being fills and transcends the entire creation. And this marvelous work of love goes on forever, for he whom we love is eternal. Whoever has the grace to appreciate the truth of what I am saying, let him take my words to heart, for to experience this love is the joy of eternal life while to lose it is eternal torment.

He who with the help of God's grace becomes aware of the will's constant movements and learns to direct them toward God will never fail to taste something of heaven's joy even in this life and, certainly in the next, he will savor it fully.[5] Now do you see why I rouse you to this spiritual work? You would have taken to it naturally had man not sinned, for man was created to love and everything else was created to make love possible.[6] Nevertheless, by the work of contemplative love man will be healed.[7] Failing in this work he sinks deeper into sin further and further from God, but by persevering in it he gradually rises from sin and grows in divine intimacy.

Therefore, be attentive to time and the way you spend it. Nothing is more precious. This is evident when you recall that in one tiny moment heaven may be gained or lost. God, the master of time, never gives the future. He gives only the present, moment by moment, for this is the law of the created order, and God will not contradict himself in his creation. Time is for man, not man for time. God, the Lord of nature, will never anticipate man's choices which follow one after another in time. Man will not be able to excuse himself at the last judgment, saying to God: "You overwhelmed me with the future when I was only capable of living in the present."

But now I see that you are discouraged and are saying to yourself: "What am I to do? If all he says is true, how shall I justify my past? I am twenty-four years old and until this moment I have scarcely noticed time at all. What is worse, I could not repair the past even if I wanted to, for according to his teaching such a task is impossible to me by nature even with the help of ordinary grace. Besides I know very well that in the future, either through frailty or laziness, I will probably not be any more attentive to the present moment than I have been in the past. I am completely discouraged. Please help me for the love of Jesus."

Well have you said "for the love of Jesus." For it is in his love that you will find help. In love all things are shared and so if you love Jesus, everything of his is yours. As God he is the creator and dispenser of time; as man he consciously mastered time; as God and man he is the rightful judge of men and their use of time. Bind yourself to Jesus, therefore, in faith and love, so that belonging to him you may share all he has and enter the fellowship of those who love him. This is the communion of the blessed and these will be your friends: our Lady, St. Mary, who was full of grace at every moment; the angels, who are unable to waste time; and all the blessed in heaven and on earth, who through the grace of Jesus employ every moment in love.[8] See, here is your strength. Understand what I am saying and be heartened. But remember, I warn you of one thing above all. No one can claim true fellowship with Jesus, his Mother, the angels, and the saints, unless he does all in his power with the help of grace to be mindful

51

of time. For he must do his share however slight to strengthen the fellowship as it strengthens him.

And so do not neglect this contemplative work. Try also to appreciate its wonderful effects in your own spirit. When it is genuine it is simply a spontaneous desire springing suddenly toward God like spark from fire.[9] It is amazing how many loving desires arise from the spirit of a person who is accustomed to this work. And yet, perhaps only one of these will be completely free from attachment to some created thing. Or again, no sooner has a man turned toward God in love when through human frailty he finds himself distracted by the remembrance of some created thing or some daily care. But no matter. No harm is done; for such a person quickly returns to deep recollection.

And now we come to the difference between the contemplative work and its counterfeits such as daydreaming, fantasizing, or subtle reasoning. These originate in a conceited, curious, or romantic mind whereas the blind stirring of love springs from a sincere and humble heart. Pride, curiosity, and daydreaming must be sternly checked if the contemplative work is to be authentically conceived in singleness of heart. Some will probably hear about this work and suppose that by their own ingenious efforts they can achieve it. They are likely to strain their mind and imagination unnaturally only to produce a false work which is neither human nor divine. Truly, such a person is dangerously deceived. And I fear that unless God intervenes with a miracle inspiring him to abandon these practices and humbly seek reliable counsel he will most certainly fall into mental aberrations or some great spiritual evil of the devil's devising. Then he risks losing both body and soul eternally. For the love of God, therefore, be careful in this work and never strain your mind or imagination, for truly you will not succeed this way. Leave these faculties at peace.[10]

Do not suppose that because I have spoken of darkness and of a cloud I have in mind the clouds you see in an overcast sky or the darkness of your house when your candle fails. If

I had, you could with a little imagination picture the summer skies breaking through the clouds or a clear light brightening the dark winter. But this isn't what I mean at all so forget this sort of nonsense. When I speak of darkness, I mean the absence of knowledge.[11] If you are unable to understand something or if you have forgotten it, are you not in the dark as regards this thing? You cannot see it with your mind's eye. Well, in the same way, I have not said "cloud," but *cloud of unknowing*. For it is a darkness of unknowing that lies between you and your God.

CHAPTER 5

That during contemplative prayer all created things and their works must be buried beneath the cloud of forgetting.

If you wish to enter into this cloud, to be at home in it, and to take up the contemplative work of love as I urge you to, there is something else you must do. Just as the *cloud of unknowing* lies above you, between you and your God, so you must fashion a *cloud of forgetting* beneath you, between you and every created thing. The *cloud of unknowing* will perhaps leave you with the feeling that you are far from God. But no, if it is authentic, only the absence of a *cloud of forgetting* keeps you from him now. Every time I say "all creatures," I refer not only to every created thing but also to all their circumstances and activities. I make no exception. You are to concern yourself with no creature whether material or spiritual nor with their situation and doings whether good or ill. To put it briefly, during this work you must abandon them all beneath the *cloud of forgetting*.

For although at certain times and in certain circumstances it is necessary and useful to dwell on the particular situation and activity of people and things, during this work it is

53

almost useless. Thinking and remembering are forms of spiritual understanding in which the eye of the spirit is opened and closed upon things as the eye of a marksman is on his target. But I tell you that everything you dwell upon during this work becomes an obstacle to union with God.[1] For if your mind is cluttered with these concerns there is no room for him.

Yes, and with all due reverence, I go so far as to say that it is equally useless to think you can nourish your contemplative work by considering God's attributes, his kindness or his dignity; or by thinking about our Lady, the angels, or the saints; or about the joys of heaven, wonderful as these will be. I believe that this kind of activity is no longer of any use to you. Of course, it is laudable to reflect upon God's kindness and to love and praise him for it; yet it is far better to let your mind rest in the awareness of him in his naked existence and to love and praise him for what he is in himself.

CHAPTER 6

A short explanation of contemplation in the form of a dialogue.

Now you say, "How shall I proceed to think of God as he is in himself?" To this I can only reply, "I do not know."

With this question you bring me into the very darkness and *cloud of unknowing* that I want you to enter. A man may know completely and ponder thoroughly every created thing and its works, yes, and God's works, too, but not God himself. Thought cannot comprehend God. And so, I prefer to abandon all I can know, choosing rather to love him whom I cannot know.[1] Though we cannot know him we can love him. By love he may be touched and embraced, never by thought. Of course, we do well at times to ponder God's majesty or

54

kindness for the insight these meditations may bring. But in the real contemplative work you must set all this aside and cover it over with a *cloud of forgetting*. Then let your loving desire, gracious and devout, step bravely and joyfully beyond it and reach out to pierce the darkness above.[2] Yes, beat upon that thick *cloud of unknowing* with the dart of your loving desire and do not cease come what may.

CHAPTER 7

How a person should conduct himself during prayer with regard to all thoughts, especially those arising from curiosity and natural intelligence.

It is inevitable that ideas will arise in your mind and try to distract you in a thousand ways. They will question you saying, "What are you looking for, what do you want?" To all of them you must reply, "God alone I seek and desire, only him."

If they ask, "Who is this God?", tell them that he is the God who created you, redeemed you, and brought you to this work. Say to your thoughts, "You are powerless to grasp him. Be still." Dispel them by turning to Jesus with loving desire. Don't be surprised if your thoughts seem holy and valuable for prayer. Probably you will find yourself thinking about the wonderful qualities of Jesus, his sweetness, his love, his graciousness, his mercy. But if you pay attention to these ideas they will have gained what they wanted of you, and will go on chattering until they divert you even more to the thought of his passion. Then will come ideas about his great kindness, and if you keep listening they will be delighted. Soon you will be thinking about your sinful life and perhaps in this connection you will recall some place where you have lived in the past, until suddenly, before you know it, your mind is completely scattered.

And yet, they were not bad thoughts. Actually, they were good and holy thoughts, so valuable, in fact, that anyone who expects to advance without having meditated often on his own sinfulness, the Passion of Christ, and the kindness, goodness, and dignity of God, will most certainly go astray and fail in his purpose. But a person who has long pondered these things must eventually leave them behind beneath a *cloud of forgetting* if he hopes to pierce the *cloud of unknowing* that lies between him and his God. So whenever you feel drawn by grace to the contemplative work and are determined to do it, simply raise your heart to God with a gentle stirring of love. Think only of God, the God who created you, redeemed you, and guided you to this work. Allow no other ideas about God to enter your mind. Yet even this is too much. A naked intent toward God, the desire for him alone, is enough.[1]

If you want to gather all your desire into one simple word that the mind can easily retain, choose a short word rather than a long one. A one-syllable word such as "God" or "love" is best. But choose one that is meaningful to you. Then fix it in your mind so that it will remain there come what may. This word will be your defense in conflict and in peace. Use it to beat upon the cloud of darkness above you and to subdue all distractions, consigning them to the *cloud of forgetting* beneath you. Should some thought go on annoying you demanding to know what you are doing, answer with this one word alone. If your mind begins to intellectualize over the meaning and connotations of this little word, remind yourself that its value lies in its simplicity. Do this and I assure you these thoughts will vanish. Why? Because you have refused to develop them with arguing.

CHAPTER 8

A good exposition of certain doubts that may arise con-
cerning contemplation; that a man's curiosity, learning,
and natural intelligence must be abandoned in this work;
of the distinction between the degrees and parts of the
active and contemplative life.

But now you say to me, "How am I to judge these ideas that
press in upon me as I pray? Are they good or evil? And if
they are evil, I am amazed because they arouse my devotion
so much. At times they are a real comfort and even make me
weep for sorrow at Christ's Passion or my own sinfulness.
For other reasons, too, I am inclined to believe that these
holy meditations do me a great deal of good. So if they are
not evil but actually good, I don't understand why you advise
me to abandon them beneath a *cloud of forgetting*."

Now these are very good questions and I will try my best
to answer them. First of all, you want to know what kind of
thoughts they are, pretending to be so helpful. To this I say:
these are the clear ideas of natural intelligence which reason
conceives in your mind. As to whether they are good or evil,
I must insist that they are always good in themselves, for
your intelligence is a reflection of the divine intelligence. But
what you do with them may be either good or evil. Certainly
they are good when with God's grace they help you understand your sinfulness, the Passion of Christ, the kindness of
God, or the marvels that he works throughout creation. It is
little wonder that such reflections deepen your devotion. But
they become evil when, inflated by pride, intellectual curiosity, and egoism, they corrupt your mind. For then you have
put aside the humble mind of a scholar, a master of theology
and asceticism, to become like the proud scholars of the devil,

experts in vanities and lies. This I say as a warning for everyone. Natural intelligence is turned to evil whenever it is filled with pride and unnecessary curiosity about worldly affairs and human vanities, or when it selfishly covets worldly dignities, riches, empty pleasures, or flattery.

Now, you ask, if then these thoughts are not only good in themselves but may also be used to good advantage why must they be abandoned beneath a *cloud of forgetting?* To answer this will require some explanation. Let me begin by saying that in the Church there are two kinds of life, the active and the contemplative. The active life is lower, and the contemplative life is higher. Within the active life there are two degrees, a lower and a higher, and within the contemplative life there are also two degrees, a lower and a higher. But these two lives are so complementary that although they are quite different from one another, neither can exist completely independent of the other. For the higher degree of the active life flows into the lower degree of the contemplative life so that, no matter how active a person may be, he is also at the same time partially contemplative; and when he is as fully contemplative as he can be in this life, he remains to some extent active also.

The active life is such that it begins and ends on earth. The contemplative life, however, may indeed begin on earth but it will continue without end into eternity. This is because the contemplative life is *Mary's part which shall never be taken away.* The active life is troubled and busy about many things but the contemplative life *sits in peace with the one thing necessary.*[1]

In the lower degree of the active life a person does well to busy himself with good deeds and the works of mercy. In the higher degree of the active life (which merges with the lower degree of the contemplative life) he begins to meditate on the things of the spirit. This is when he ought to ponder with sorrow the sinfulness of man so as to enter into the Passion of Christ and the sufferings of his saints with pity and compassion. It is a time when one grows in appreciation of God's kindness and his gifts, and begins to praise and thank him for the wonderful ways he works in all his creation. But in the higher degree of contemplation—such as we know it in this life—all is darkness and a *cloud of unknowing*. Here one turns to God with a burning desire for himself alone and rests in the blind awareness of his naked being.[2]

The activities of the lower degree of the active life in themselves leave much of man's natural human potential untapped. At this stage he lives, as it were, outside himself or beneath himself. As he advances to the higher degree of the active life (which merges with the lower degree of the contemplative life) he becomes increasingly interior, living more from the depths of himself and becoming, therefore, more fully human. But in the higher degree of the contemplative life, he transcends himself because he achieves by grace what is beyond him by nature. For now he is bound to God spiritually in a communion of love and desire.[3] Experience teaches that it is necessary to set aside for a time the works of the lower degree of the active life in order to go on to the higher degree of the active life, which, as we said, flows into the lower degree of the contemplative life. In the same way, there comes a time when it is necessary to set aside these works also in order to go on to the higher degree of the contemplative life. And as it is wrong for a person who sits in meditation to be thinking about the things he has done or will do regardless how good and worthwhile they may be in themselves, likewise it is wrong for a person who ought to be busy with the contemplative work in the darkness of the *cloud of unknowing* to let ideas about God, his wonderful gifts, his kindness, or his works distract him from attentiveness to God himself. It is beside the point to say that they are good thoughts full of comfort and delight. They have no place here![4]

This is why I urge you to dismiss every clever or subtle thought no matter how holy or valuable. Cover it over with a thick *cloud of forgetting* because in this life only love can touch God as he is in himself, never knowledge.[5] As long as we live in these mortal bodies the keenness of our intellect remains dulled by material limitations whenever it deals with spiritual realities and most especially God. Our reasoning, therefore, is never pure thought and without the assistance of divine mercy it would lead us deep into error.

CHAPTER 9

That the most sublime thoughts are more hindrance than help during the time of contemplative prayer.

So then, you must reject all clear conceptualizations whenever they arise, as they inevitably will, during the blind work of contemplative love. If you do not conquer them they will surely conquer you. For when you most desire to be alone with God, they will slip into your mind with such stealth that only constant vigilance will detect them. Be sure that if you are occupied with something less than God, you place it above you for the time being and create a barrier between yourself and God. Therefore, firmly reject all clear ideas however pious or delightful. For I tell you this, one loving blind desire for God alone is more valuable in itself, more pleasing to God and to the saints, more beneficial to your own growth, and more helpful to your friends, both living and dead, than anything else you could do.[1] And you are more blessed to experience the interior affection of this love within the darkness of the *cloud of unknowing* than to contemplate the angels and saints or to hear the mirth and melody of their heavenly festival.

Does this surprise you? That is only because you have not experienced it for yourself. For when you do, as I certainly believe you will with God's grace, you will understand. Of course, it is impossible in this life to see and possess God fully

60

but, with his grace and in his own time, it is possible to taste something of him as he is in himself. And so with great longing for him enter into this cloud. Or rather, I should say, let God awaken your longing and draw you to himself in this cloud while you strive with the help of his grace to forget everything else.[2]

Remember, if the clear ideas which you reject can annoy and distract you from the Lord and prevent you from experiencing his love, how much more those which you willfully cultivate. And if the thought of a particular saint or some purely spiritual reality creates an obstacle to this work, how much more the thought of mortal man or some material or worldly concern. I do not say that these thoughts, either deliberate or indeliberate, are evil in themselves. God forbid that you should misunderstand me. No, what I have stressed is that they are more hindrance than help.[3] For surely if you are seeking God alone, you will never rest contented with anything less than God.

CHAPTER 10

How a man shall know when his thoughts are sinful; of the difference between mortal and venial sins.

Thoughts about mortal men and material or worldly things are another matter. It will happen that unlawful thoughts regarding them will spring suddenly into your mind without your consent. There is no sin in this, for it is not your fault but happens as the result of original sin. Although you were cleansed of original sin in baptism, you remain burdened with its consequences. Just the same you are obliged to reject these thoughts at once, for your human nature is weak and if you do not, you may find yourself stirred to love or hatred, depending on the associations they conjure up. If it is

61

a pleasurable thought or recalls some past pleasure, you may find yourself consenting to the delight of it; if it is a painful thought or recalls some painful memory, you may yield to anger. Consent like this is a deadly sin for one who is already in a state of deadly sin by reason of a fundamental choice against the good. But for you or for anyone who has sincerely renounced the world, it is only venial sin. In choosing your present way of life you made a radical commitment to God and this remains despite a temporary lapse. Your full consent is lacking and so for you it is a lesser sin. Nevertheless, if you allow your thoughts to go unchecked to the point where you willingly dwell on them with full consent, then you do commit a deadly sin. For it is a deadly sin when, with full understanding and consent, you dwell on the thought of any person or thing which stirs your heart to one of the seven deadly sins.

If you brood over an injury, past or present, you will soon feel the painful desire and thirst for revenge. This is the sin of *Anger*. Or should you conceive an evil disdain for another and the kind of hatred for him full of spite and rash judgment, you have fallen into *Envy*. If you yield to a feeling of weariness and boredom for good works, it is called *Sloth*. If the thought which comes to you (or which you invite) is full of human conceit regarding your honor, your intelligence, your gifts of grace, your status, talents, or beauty and, if you willingly rest in it with delight, it is the sin of *Pride*. If it is a thought of some material thing, that is, of wealth or property or other earthly goods that people strive to possess and call their own and, if you dwell on it with desire, it is the sin of *Covetousness*. If you yield to inordinate desire for delicacies of food or drink or for any of the delights of taste, it is called *Gluttony*. And finally, illicit desire for carnal indulgence or for the favor and flattery of others is called *Lust*.

If your vagrant thoughts recall any pleasure, past or present, and if you rest in it letting it take root in your heart and feed your carnal desire, you are in danger of being overwhelmed by the delight of passion. Soon you will think that you possess all you could ever want and that this pleasure will satisfy you perfectly.

CHAPTER 11

That a man should strictly appraise his thoughts and inclinations and avoid a careless attitude about venial sin.

I do not say all this because I am worried that you or any other person of prayer is actually burdened with the guilt of sins like these. My purpose is to impress on you the importance of weighing your thoughts and desires as they arise, for you must learn to reject the least of them that might lead you to sin. I warn you that a person who fails in vigilance and control of his thoughts, even though they are not sinful in their first movements, will eventually grow careless about small sins. It is impossible to avoid all faults and failings in this life but carelessness about deliberate small sins is intolerable to the true seeker of perfection. For usually negligence about slight sins opens the door to the likelihood of deadly sin.

CHAPTER 12

That in contemplation sin is destroyed and every kind of goodness is nourished.

And so to stand firmly and avoid pitfalls, keep to the path you are on. Let your longing relentlessly beat upon the *cloud of unknowing* that lies between you and your God. Pierce that cloud with the keen shaft of your love, spurn the thought

63

of anything less than God, and do not give up this work for anything. For the contemplative work of love by itself will eventually heal you of all the roots of sin.[1] Fast as much as you like, watch far into the night, rise long before dawn, discipline your body, and if it were permitted—which it is not —put out your eyes, tear out your tongue, plug up your ears and nose, and cut off your limbs; yes, chastise your body with every discipline and you would still gain nothing. The desire and tendency toward sin would remain in your heart.

What is more, if you wept in constant sorrow for your sins and Christ's Passion and pondered unceasingly on the joys of heaven, do you think it would do you any good? Much good, I am sure. You would profit no doubt and grow in grace but in comparison with the blind stirring of love, all this is very little. For the contemplative work of love is the best part, belonging to Mary. It is perfectly complete by itself while all these disciplines and exercises are of little value without it.

The work of love not only heals the roots of sin, but nurtures practical goodness. When it is authentic you will be sensitive to every need and respond with a generosity unspoiled by selfish intent. Anything you attempt to do without this love will certainly be imperfect, for it is sure to be marred by ulterior motives.

Genuine goodness is a matter of habitually acting and responding appropriately in each situation, as it arises, moved always by the desire to please God.[2] He alone is the pure source of all goodness and if a person is motivated by something else besides God, even though God is first, then his virtue is imperfect. This is evident in the case of two virtues in particular, humility and brotherly love. Whoever acquires these habits of mind and manner needs no others, for he will possess everything.[3]

CHAPTER 13

Of the nature of humility; when it is perfect and when it is imperfect.

Let us then consider the virtue of humility so that you will understand why it is perfect when God alone is its source and why it is imperfect when it arises from any other source even though God might be the principal one. But first I will try to explain what humility is in itself and then the difference will be easier to grasp.

A man is humble when he stands in the truth with a knowledge and appreciation for himself as he really is. And actually, anyone who saw and experienced himself as he really and truly is would have no difficulty being humble, for two things would become very clear to him. In the first place, he would see clearly the degradation, misery, and weakness of the human condition resulting from original sin. From these effects of original sin man will never be entirely free in this life, no matter how holy he becomes. In the second place, he would recognize the transcendent goodness of God as he is in himself and his overflowing, superabundant love for man. Before such goodness and love nature trembles, sages stammer like fools, and the saints and angels are blinded with glory. So overwhelming is this revelation of God's nature that if his power did not sustain them, I dare not think what might happen.

The humility engendered by this experiential knowledge of God's goodness and love I call perfect, because it is an attitude which man will retain even in eternity. But the humility arising from a realistic grasp of the human condition I call imperfect, for not only will it pass away at death with its cause but even in this life it will not always be operative. For sometimes people well advanced in the contemplative life will receive such grace from God that they will be suddenly and completely taken out of themselves and neither remember nor care whether they are holy or sinful. Proficient contemplatives may experience this more or less frequently according to God's wisdom, but in any case it is, I believe, a passing phenomenon. During such a time, however, though they may lose all concern for their sinfulness or virtue, they do not lose the sense of God's immense love and goodness and therefore, they have perfect humility. On the other hand, when the first motive is operative, even in a secondary way, they have only imperfect humility. Nevertheless, I am not suggesting that the first motive be abandoned. God forbid that you should misunderstand me, for I am convinced that it is both profitable and necessary in this life.

CHAPTER 14

That in this life imperfect humility must precede perfect humility.

Although I speak of imperfect humility it is not because I place little value on true self-knowledge. Should all the saints and angels of heaven join with all the members of the Church on earth, both religious and lay, at every degree of Christian holiness and pray for my growth in humility, I am certain that it would not profit me as much nor bring me to the perfection of this virtue as quickly as a little self-knowledge. Indeed, it is altogether impossible to arrive at perfect humility without it.

And therefore, do not shrink from the sweat and toil involved in gaining real self-knowledge, for I am sure that when you have acquired it you will very soon come to an experiential knowledge of God's goodness and love. Not a complete knowledge, of course, for that is not possible to man; not even as complete as what you will possess in the joy of eternity but certainly as complete a knowledge as is possible to man in this life.

My purpose in explaining the two kinds of humility is not to set you in pursuit of the perfect while neglecting the imperfect. No, and I trust you will never do this. My intention is simply to help you appreciate the exalted dignity of the contemplative work of love, in comparison to any other possible with grace. For the secret love of a pure heart pressing upon that dark *cloud of unknowing* between you and your God in a hidden yet certain way includes in itself perfect humility without the help of particular or clear ideas.[1] Also I wanted you to appreciate the excellence of perfect humility so that you might keep it before your heart as a spur to your love. This is important for both of us. And finally, I have troubled to explain all this because I believe that just knowing about perfect humility will in itself make you more humble. For I often think that ignorance of humility's two degrees occasions a good deal of pride. It is just possible that a little taste of what I have called imperfect humility might lead you to believe that you were already perfectly humble. But you would be badly deceived and, what is more, have actually fallen into the foul mire of conceit. And so, be diligent in striving for this virtue in all its perfection. When a person experiences it, he will not sin, then nor long afterward.

A proof that those who think the most perfect motive for humility is the realization of man's wretchedness are in error.

Believe me when I say that there is such a thing as perfect humility and that with God's grace it can be yours in this life. I insist on this because some are erroneously teaching that there is no greater humility than that occasioned by the thought of the unhappy human condition and the memory of one's sinful past.

I willingly concede that for those who are accustomed to habitual sin (as I myself have been) this is very true. And until the great rust of deadly sin is rubbed away in the Sacrament of Penance, nothing is more necessary and valuable in teaching humility than the thought of our miserable state and our former sins. But this attitude is not authentic for those who have never sinned greviously, with full knowledge and consent. They are like innocent children having only fallen through frailty and ignorance. Yet even these innocents, especially if they have set out on the way of contemplative prayer, have reason to be humble. We too, after having made proper satisfaction and amendment for our sins in confession and having moreover felt drawn by grace to contemplative prayer, shall certainly still have reason to be humble. Something far transcending the imperfect motive I mentioned earlier will keep us humble. For God's goodness and love is a reason as far above self-knowledge as our Lady's life is above the life of the most sinful penitent in Holy Church; or the life of Christ is above that of any other human being; or the life of an angel who cannot experience human weakness is above the life of the weakest man on earth.

If there were no other reason for humility besides the poverty of the human condition, then I would wonder why those who have never experienced the corruption of sin should be humble. For surely our Lord Jesus Christ, our Lady, and the saints and the angels of heaven are forever free of sin and its effects. Yet our Lord Jesus Christ himself calls us in the Gospel to the perfection of every virtue when he says that we are to be perfect by grace as he is by nature. And so this must include the virtue of humility.[1]

CHAPTER 16

That a sinner truly converted and called to contemplation comes to perfection most quickly through contemplation; that it is the surest way to obtain God's forgiveness from sin.

No matter how grievously a man has sinned, he can repent and amend his life. And if he feels God's grace drawing him on to a contemplative life (having faithfully followed the guidance of his spiritual father and counselor), let no one dare call him presumptuous for reaching out to God in the darkness of that *cloud of unknowing* with the humble desire of his love. For did not our Lord say to Mary, who represents all repentant sinners called to contemplation: "Your sins are forgiven."[1] Do you think he said this only because she was so mindful of her past sins; or because of the humility she felt at the sight of her misery; or because her sorrow was so great? No, it was because "she loved much."

Mark this well. For in this you can see how powerful with God that secret contemplative love is. It is more powerful, I can assure you, than anything else.[2] Yet at the same time, Mary was certainly filled with remorse, wept much for her past sins, and was deeply humiliated at the thought of her wretchedness. In the same way, we who have been such miserable, habitual sinners all our lives should also sincerely regret our past and be thoroughly humbled remembering that unhappy state.

But how? Surely Mary's way is best. Truly she never ceased to feel an abiding sorrow for her sins and all her life carried them like a great secret burden in her heart. Yet the Scriptures testify that her deepest sorrow was not so much for her evil deeds as for her failure to love. Yes, and for this she languished with painful longing and sorrow almost to the point of death, for although her love was very great it seemed little to her. Don't be surprised at this. It is the way of all true lovers.[3] The more they love the more they desire to love. In her heart she knew with absolute certainty that she was the most wretched of all sinners. She realized that her evil deeds had cut her off from the God she loved so much and because of that she languished now, sick for her failure to love. And so what did she do? Do you suppose she then descended from the heights of her great desire into the depths of her evil life searching that foul mire and cesspool for her sins, inspecting them one by one in all their minute details in order to tabulate her sorrow and tears more efficiently? She certainly did not. Why? Because God himself, in the depths of her spirit, taught her by grace the futility of this approach. She could sooner have roused herself to new sins than secure forgiveness of her past with tears alone.

Therefore, she fastened her love and longing on to that *cloud of unknowing* and learned to love him without seeing him in the clear light of reason or feeling his presence in the sensible delight of devotion.[4] So absorbed did she become in love that often she forgot whether she had been sinner or innocent. Yes, and I think that she became so enamored of the Lord's divinity that she scarcely noticed the beauty of his human presence as he sat there before her, speaking and teaching. From the Gospel account it would seem that she became oblivious of everything both material and spiritual.[5]

CHAPTER 17

*That a true contemplative will not meddle in the active
life nor with what goes on about him, not even to defend
himself against those who criticize him.*

In the Gospel of St. Luke we read that our Lord came to
Martha's house and while she set about at once to prepare
his meal, her sister Mary did nothing but sit at his feet. She
was so intent upon listening to him that she paid no attention to what Martha was doing. Now certainly Martha's chores
were holy and important. (Indeed, they are the works of the
first degree of the active life.) But Mary was unconcerned
about them. Neither did she notice our Lord's human bearing, the beauty of his mortal body, or the sweetness of his
human voice and conversation, although this would have been
a holier and better work. (It represents the second degree of
the active life and the first degree of the contemplative life.)
But she forgot all of this and was totally absorbed in the highest wisdom of God concealed in the obscurity of his humanity.

Mary turned to Jesus with all the love of her heart, unmoved by what she saw or heard spoken and done about her.
She sat there in perfect stillness with her heart's secret, joyous love intent upon that *cloud of unknowing* between her
and her God. For as I have said before, there never has been
and there never will be a creature so pure or so deeply immersed in the loving contemplation of God who does not
approach him in this life through that lofty and marvelous
cloud of unknowing.[1] And it was to this very cloud that Mary
directed the hidden yearning of her loving heart. Why? Because it is the best and holiest part of the contemplative life
possible to man and she would not relinquish it for anything
on earth. Even when Martha complained to Jesus about her,

71

scolding him for not bidding her to get up and help with the work, Mary remained there quite still and untroubled, showing not the least resentment against Martha for her grumbling. But this is not surprising really, for she was utterly absorbed in another work, all unknown to Martha, and she did not have time to notice her sister or defend herself.[2]

My friend, do you see that this whole incident concerning Jesus and the two sisters was intended as a lesson for active and contemplative persons of the Church in every age? Mary represents the contemplative life and all contemplative persons ought to model their lives on hers. Martha represents the active life and all active persons should take her as their guide.

CHAPTER 18

How to this day active people will criticize contemplatives through ignorance, even as Martha criticized Mary.

Just as Martha complained about Mary so in every age active persons have complained about contemplatives. How often it happens that the grace of contemplation will awaken in people of every walk and station of life, both religious and lay alike. But when after searching their own conscience and seeking reliable counsel they decide to devote themselves entirely to contemplation, their family and friends descend upon them in a storm of fury and criticism severely reproving them for idleness.[1] These people will unearth every kind of dire tale both true and false about others who have taken up this way of life and ended up in terrible evils. Assuredly, they have nothing good to tell.

It is true that many who seemingly left worldly vanities behind have afterward followed evil ways. There is always that danger. These people who ought to have entered God's

72

service as his contemplatives became instead slaves of the devil and the devil's contemplatives because they refused to listen to the counsel of authentic spiritual guides. They became hypocrites or heretics and fell into frenzies and other wickedness which led them to slander Holy Church. I hesitate to go on about this right now lest I obscure our subject. But later on, God willing, if I see it is necessary, I shall tell you some of the causes and circumstances of their downfall. Let us leave the matter for the time being and continue with our subject.

CHAPTER 19

A brief apology by the author in which he teaches that contemplatives should excuse active people who complain about them.

Perhaps you feel that I have insulted Martha, one of God's special friends, by comparing her to the worldly people who criticize contemplatives or by comparing them to her. Really, I meant no offense to either of them. God forbid that I should say anything in this book to condemn any of God's friends of whatever degree of holiness, let alone one of his saints. For actually I believe we should excuse Martha for complaining, considering the time and circumstances of the incident. She did not realize then what Mary was doing. It is not surprising either, for I doubt that she had so much as heard of perfection like this. Besides, she was courteous and brief in her complaint and so I believe she should be completely excused.

Likewise I think that worldly-minded critics who find fault with contemplatives should also be excused on account of their ignorance, though they are sometimes rude besides. As certainly as Martha was ignorant of what she was saying when she protested to the Lord, so these people understand little or nothing about the contemplative life. The ardor of young God-seekers baffles them. They cannot understand how these young people can cast aside careers and opportunity and set out in simple goodness and sincerity to be God's special friends. I am certain if any of this made sense to them, they would not carry on as they do. And therefore, I believe we should excuse them. They have experienced only one way of living—their own—and can imagine no other. Besides, when I recall the ways I have failed through ignorance, I feel I should have a kindly tolerance for others. Otherwise I would not be treating them as I wish to be treated myself.

CHAPTER 20

That in a spiritual way Almighty God will defend all those who for love of him will not abandon their contemplation to defend themselves.

I think that those striving to be contemplative should not only pardon all who complain about them, but be so occupied with their own work that they do not even notice what is said or done around them. That is what Mary Magdalene did and she is our model. If we follow her example Jesus will surely do for us what he did for her.

And what was that? You recall that Martha urged Jesus to reprimand Mary; to tell her to get up and help with the work. But our blessed Lord Jesus Christ, who discerned the secret thoughts of every heart, understood perfectly that Mary was deep in loving contemplation of his divinity and so he himself took her part. With a gentle courtesy befitting his goodness, he answered for her because for love of him she would not leave him long enough to answer for herself. And what did he say? Martha had appealed to him as judge but

74

he answered as more than a judge. He spoke as Mary's legal defender because she loved him so much. "Martha, Martha," he said. He called her name twice to be certain that she heard him and would stop long enough to pay attention to what he was about to say. "You are busy and troubled about many things." This indicates that active persons will always be busy and concerned about countless diverse affairs pertaining first of all to themselves and then to their fellow Christians as love requires. He wanted Martha to realize that her work was important and valuable to her spiritual development. Lest she conclude, however, that it was the highest work possible, he added: "But only one thing is necessary." And what do you suppose this one thing is? Surely he was referring to the work of loving and praising God for his own sake. There is no work greater. Finally, he wanted Martha to understand that it is not possible to be entirely dedicated to this work and the active work at the same time. Everyday concerns and the contemplative life cannot be perfectly combined though they may be united in some incomplete fashion. To make this clear he added: "Mary has chosen the best part which shall never be taken from her." For the work of perfect love which begins here on earth is the same as that love which is eternal life; they are but one.

CHAPTER 21

A true explanation of the Gospel passage: Mary has chosen the best part.

"Mary has chosen the best part." What does this mean? Whenever we speak of the best, we imply a good and a better. The best is the superlative degree. What then are the options from which Mary chose the best? They are not three ways of life since Holy Church only speaks of two, the active

75

and the contemplative. No, the deeper meaning of the Gospel story from St. Luke which we have just considered is that Martha represents the active life and Mary the contemplative life, the first of which is absolutely necessary for salvation. So when a choice narrows down to two, one of them may not be called best.

Nevertheless, although the active and the contemplative are the two ways of life in Holy Church, yet within them, taken as a whole, there are three parts, three ascending stages. These we have already discussed,[1] but I will briefly summarize them here. The first stage is the good and upright Christian life in which love is predominantly active in the corporal works of mercy. In the second, a person begins to meditate on spiritual truths regarding his own sinfulness, the Passion of Christ, and the joys of eternity. The first way is good but the second is better, for here the active and contemplative life begin to converge. They merge in a sort of spiritual kinship, becoming sisters like Martha and Mary. This is as far as an active person may advance in contemplation except for the occasional intervention of special grace. And to this middle ground a contemplative may return—but no farther—to take up some activity. He should not do so, however, except on rare occasions and at the demand of great need.

In the third stage a person enters the dark *cloud of unknowing* where in secret and alone he centers all his love on God. The first stage is good, the second is better, but the third is best of all. This is the best part belonging to Mary. It is surely obvious now why our Lord did not say to Martha, "Mary has chosen the best life." There are only two ways of life and, as I said, when a choice is only between two one may not be called best. But our Lord says, "Mary has chosen the best *part* and it shall not be taken from her."

The first and second parts are good and holy but they will cease with the passing of this mortal life. For in eternity there will be no need for the works of mercy as there is now. People will not hunger or thirst or die of cold or be sick, homeless, and captive. No one will need Christian burial for no one will die. In heaven it will no longer be fitting to mourn for our sins or for Christ's Passion. So then, if grace is calling you to choose the third part, choose it with Mary. Or rather let me put it this way. If God is calling you to the third part, reach out for it; work for it with all your heart. It shall never be taken from you, for it will never end. Though it begins on earth, it is eternal.

Let the words of the Lord be our reply to active persons who complain about us. Let him speak for us as he did for Mary when he said, "Martha, Martha." He is saying, "Listen, all you who live the active life. Be diligent in the works of the first and second parts, working now in one, now in another. Or if you are so inclined, courageously undertake both together. But do not interfere with my contemplative friends, for you do not understand what afflicts them. Leave them in peace. Do not begrudge them the leisure of the third and best part which is Mary's."[2]

CHAPTER 22

Of the wonderful love Christ had for Mary Magdalene, who represents all sinners truly converted and called to contemplation.

Sweet was the love between Mary and Jesus. How she loved him! How much more he loved her! Do not take the Gospel account lightly as if it were some superficial tale. It depicts their relationship in utter truth. Reading it, who could fail to see that she loved him intensely, withholding nothing of her love and refusing the comfort of anything less than his love in return. This is the same Mary who sought him weeping at the tomb that first Easter morning. The angels spoke to her so gently then. "Do not weep, Mary," they said. "For the Lord whom you seek is risen as he said. He is going on before

77

you into Galilee. There you will see him with his disciples, as he promised."[1] But even angels were powerless to reassure her or stop her tears. Mere angels could hardly comfort one who had set out to find the King of Angels.[2]

Shall I go on? Surely anyone who studies the Scripture will find many instances of Mary's total love for Christ recorded there for our benefit. They will confirm all I have been saying. In fact, one would think they had been written specifically for contemplatives. And so they were, for anyone discerning enough to see. Anyone who recognizes in our Lord's wonderful personal love for Mary Magdalene the marvelous and matchless love he has for all sinners sincerely repentant and dedicated to contemplation will realize why he could tolerate no one—not even her sister—to speak against her without coming to her defense himself. Yes, and more did he do. For on another occasion he even rebuked his host, Simon the Leper, in his own house, for merely thinking harshly of her. Great indeed was his love; truly it was unsurpassed.

CHAPTER 23

That in a spiritual way God will answer and provide for all those who will not leave their contemplation to answer and provide for themselves.

I assure you that if with God's grace and reliable counsel we strive wholeheartedly to pattern our love and our life after Mary Magdalene's, our Lord will defend us as he did her. Anyone who thinks or speaks against us will feel the Lord's rebuke in the secret of his conscience. This is not to say that we shall have nothing to put up with. Certainly we shall, as Mary did. But I am saying that if we pay no attention to it, but peacefully go on with our contemplative work despite

78

criticism, just as she did, our Lord will admonish those who plague us in the depths of their hearts. If they are sincere and open people, they will no doubt feel ashamed of their thoughts or words within a few days.[1]

And just as he will see to our spiritual defense, so he will prompt others to provide us with food and clothes and life's necessities when he sees that we will not leave the work of love to see about such things for ourselves. I say this specifically to refute those who erroneously maintain that no one may devote himself to the contemplative life before he has provided for all his material needs. They say: "God sends the cow, but not by the horn."[2] But they misinterpret God and they know it. For God will never disappoint those who truly abandon worldly concerns to dedicate themselves to him. You can be certain of this: he will provide one of two things for his friends. Either they will receive an abundance of all they need or he will give them the physical stamina and a patient heart to endure want. What difference does it make which he does? It is all the same to the true contemplative. Anyone doubting this only reveals that the evil one has robbed his heart of faith or that he is not yet as wholly committed to God as he should be, despite cleverly contrived appearances to the contrary.

And so I say again to anyone who wants to become a real contemplative like Mary, let the wonderful transcendence and goodness of God teach you humility rather than the thought of your own sinfulness, for then your humility will be perfect. Attend more to the wholly otherness of God rather than to your own misery. And remember that those who are perfectly humble will lack nothing they really need, either spiritually or materially. God is theirs and he is all. Whoever possesses God, as this book attests, needs nothing else in this life.

What charity is in itself; how it is subtly and perfectly contained in contemplative love.

We have seen that perfect humility is an integral part of the contemplative's simple blind love. Wholly intent upon God, this simple love beats unceasingly upon the dark *cloud of unknowing*, leaving all discursive thought beneath the *cloud of forgetting*. Now just as contemplative love nurtures perfect humility, so it is creative of practical goodness. especially charity. For in real charity one loves God for himself alone above every created thing and he loves his fellow man because it is God's law. In the contemplative work God is loved above every creature purely and simply for his own sake. Indeed, the very heart of this work is nothing else but a naked intent toward God for his own sake.[1]

I call it a naked intent because it is utterly disinterested. In this work the perfect artisan does not seek personal gain or exemption from suffering. He desires only God and him alone.[2] He is so fascinated by the God he loves and so concerned that his will be done on earth that he neither notices nor cares about his own ease or anxiety. This is why, I believe, that in this work God is really loved perfectly and for his own sake. For a true contemplative may share with no other creature the love he owes to God.

Moreover, in contemplation the second and subsidiary command of charity is also completely fulfilled. The fruits of contemplation bear witness to this even though during the actual time of prayer the skilled contemplative has no special regard for any person in particular, whether brother or stranger, friend or enemy. In reality, no man is a stranger to him because he looks on each one as a brother. And none is his enemy. All are his friends. Even those who hurt or offend him in everyday life are as dear to him as his best friends and all the good he desires for his best friends he desires for them.

CHAPTER 25

That in the time of contemplative prayer, the perfect contemplative does not focus his attention on any person in particular.

I have already explained that during the time of this work a real contemplative does not dwell on the thought of any person in particular, neither friend, enemy, stranger, nor kin. For he who desires to become perfect in this work must forget about everything except God.

Nevertheless, through contemplation he is so growing in practical goodness and love that, when he speaks or prays with his fellow Christians at other times, the warmth of his love reaches out to them all, friend, enemy, stranger, and kin alike. If there is any partiality at all, it is more likely to be toward his enemy than toward his friend. (Not that he should ever abandon contemplation entirely—for this could not be done without great sin—but sometimes charity will demand that he descend from the heights of this work to do something for his fellow man.)

But in the contemplative work itself, he does not distinguish between friend and enemy, brother and stranger. I do not mean, however, that he will cease to feel a spontaneous affection toward a few others who are especially close to him. Of course, he will and frequently, too. This is perfectly natural and legitimate for many reasons known only to love. You will remember that Christ himself had a special love for John and Mary and Peter. The point I am making is that during the work of contemplation everyone is equally dear to him since it is God alone who stirs him to love. He loves all men plainly and nakedly for God; and he loves them as he loves himself.

All men were lost through Adam's sin but all those who by their good will manifest a desire to be saved shall be saved by Christ's redeeming death. A person deeply committed to contemplation shares in Christ's redemptive suffering, not exactly as Christ did himself, but in a manner similar to Christ's. For in true contemplation a person is one with God in a spiritual sense and does all in his power to draw others to perfect contemplation. You know that your whole body shares in the pain or the well-being felt by any of its parts, because it is a unity. In a spiritual sense, all Christians are parts of Christ's one body. He is our head and if we are in grace we are his members. On the Cross he sacrificed himself for his body, the Church. Whoever wishes to follow Christ perfectly must also be willing to expend himself in the spiritual work of love for the salvation of all his brothers and sisters in the human family. I repeat, not only for his friends and family and those most dear to him, but with universal affection he must work for the salvation of all mankind. For Christ died to save anyone who repents of his sins and seeks the mercy of God.[1]

So you see, contemplative love is so refined and integral that it includes in itself perfectly both humility and charity. For the same reasons and in the same way, it perfectly includes every other virtue as well.[2]

That without special grace or a long fidelity to ordinary grace, contemplative prayer is very difficult; that this work is possible only with grace, for it is the work of God.

So then, take up the toil of the contemplative work with wholehearted generosity. Beat upon this high *cloud of unknowing* and spurn the thought of resting. For I tell you frankly that anyone who really desires to be a contemplative will know the pain of arduous toil (unless God should intervene with special grace); he will feel keenly the cost of constant effort until he is long accustomed to this work.

But tell me, why should it be so difficult? Surely, the fervent love continually awakening in the will is not painful. No, for that is God's doing, the fruit of his almighty power. Moreover, God is always eager to work in the heart of one who has done all he can to prepare the way for his grace. Then why is this work so toilsome? The labor, of course, is in the unrelenting struggle to banish the countless distracting thoughts that plague our minds and to restrain them beneath that *cloud of forgetting* which I spoke of earlier. This is the suffering. All the struggle is on man's side in the effort he must make to prepare himself for God's action, which is the awakening of love and which he alone can do. But persevere in doing your part and I promise you that God will not fail to do his.[1]

Keep at this work faithfully then. I want to see how you get along. Don't you see how the Lord patiently supports you? Blush for shame! Bear the hardship of discipline for a short while and soon the difficulty and burden of it will abate. In the beginning you will feel tried and constrained but this is only because you do not yet experience the interior joy of this

83

work. As time goes by, however, you will feel a joyful enthusiasm for it and then it will seem light and easy indeed. Then you will feel little or no constraint, for God will sometimes work in your spirit all by himself. Yet not always nor for very long but as it seems best to him. When he does you will rejoice, and be happy to let him do as he wishes.

Then perhaps he may touch you with a ray of his divine light which will pierce the *cloud of unknowing* between you and him. He will let you glimpse something of the ineffable secrets of his divine wisdom and your affection will seem on fire with his love. I am at a loss to say more, for the experience is beyond words.[2] Even if I were able to say more I would not now. For I dare not try to describe God's grace with my crude and awkward tongue. In a word, even if I dared I would not.

But when grace awakens in a man's spirit he must do his part to respond and this I will discuss with you. There is less risk in speaking of this.[3]

CHAPTER 27

Who ought to engage in the gracious work of contemplation.

First and foremost I want to state clearly who should take up the contemplative work, when it is appropriate to do so, and how a person ought to proceed. Also I want to give you some criteria for discernment in this work.

If you ask who should take up contemplation I would reply: all those who have sincerely forsaken the world and who have set aside the concerns of the active life. These people, even if they have at one time been habitual sinners, should devote themselves to nourishing the grace of contemplative prayer.

That a man should not presume to begin contemplation until he has purified his conscience of all particular sin according to the law of the Church.

If you ask me when a person should begin the contemplative work I would answer: not until he has first purified his conscience of all particular sins in the Sacrament of Penance as the Church prescribes.

After Confession the root and ground from which evil springs will still remain in his heart despite all his efforts, but the work of love will eventually heal them totally.[1] And so a person should first cleanse his conscience in Confession. But once having done what the Church requires, he should fearlessly begin the contemplative work, yet humbly, too, realizing that he has been long in coming to it. For even those innocent of grave sin will spend their whole lives at this work because as long as we are in these mortal bodies we shall experience the impenetrable darkness of the *cloud of unknowing* between us and God.[2] Moreover, because of original sin we shall always suffer the burden of our vagrant thoughts, which will seek to divert our complete attention from God.

This is the just punishment of original sin. Before he sinned, man was master and lord of all creatures but he yielded to the evil suggestion of these creatures and disobeyed God. And now when he wishes to obey God he feels the drag of created things. Like arrogant pests they annoy him as he reaches out for God.

That a man should patiently persevere at the work of contemplation, willingly bear its sufferings, and judge no one else.

Anyone who desires to regain the purity of heart lost through sin and to win that personal wholeness beyond all pain must patiently struggle in the contemplative work and endure its toil whether he has been a habitual sinner or not. Both sinners and innocents will suffer in this work although obviously sinners will feel the suffering more. And yet it often happens that some who have been hardened, habitual sinners arrive at the perfection of this work sooner than those who have never sinned grievously. God is truly wonderful in lavishing his grace on anyone he chooses; the world stands bewildered before love like this.

And I believe that Doomsday will actually be glorious, for the goodness of God will shine clearly in all his gifts of grace. Some who are now despised and held in contempt (and who are even perhaps inveterate sinners) shall on that day reign in splendor with his saints. And perhaps some of those who have never sinned grievously and who to all appearances are pious people, venerated as gods by other men, shall find themselves in misery among the damned.

My point is that in this life no man may judge another as good or evil simply on the evidence of his deeds. The deeds themselves are another matter. These we may judge as good or evil, but not the person.

Who has the right to judge and censure the faults of others.

Yet we may ask, is there anyone who can judge another man's life?

Yes, of course, he who has the authority and responsibility for the spiritual good of others may rightfully censure the deeds of men. A man may officially receive this power through the decree and ordination of the Church, or it is possible that the Holy Spirit may privately inspire a particular individual well established in love to assume this office. But let everyone be very careful not to arrogate to himself the duty of monitoring the faults of others, for he is liable to great error. It is another matter if in contemplation a man is really inspired to speak out.

And so I warn you, think twice about passing judgment on the lives of other men. In the privacy of your own conscience judge yourself as you see fit before God or before your spiritual father, but do not meddle in the lives of others.

CHAPTER 31

How the beginners in contemplation should conduct themselves in regard to their thoughts and inclinations to sin.

When you feel that you have done your best to amend your life according to the laws of the Church, give yourself in earnest to the contemplative work. And if the memory of your past sins or the temptation to new ones should plague your mind, forming an obstacle between you and God, crush them beneath your feet and bravely step beyond them. Try to bury the thought of these deeds beneath the thick *cloud of forgetting* just as if neither you nor anyone else had ever done them. If they persist in returning, you must persist in rejecting them. In short, as often as they rise up you must put them down. If you become sorely tried you will probably begin to investigate techniques, methods, and the secret subtleties of occult crafts to help you control them, but believe me, techniques for controlling your thoughts are better learned from God through experience than from any man in this life.

CHAPTER 32

Of two spiritual devices helpful to beginners in contemplation.

All the same I will tell you a little about two techniques for handling distractions. Try them and improve on them if you can.

When distracting thoughts annoy you try to pretend that you do not even notice their presence or that they have come between you and your God. Look beyond them—over their shoulder, as it were—as if you were looking for something else, which of course you are. For beyond them, God is hidden in the dark *cloud of unknowing*. Do this and I feel sure you will soon be relieved of anxiety about them. I can vouch for the orthodoxy of this technique because in reality it amounts to a yearning for God, a longing to see and taste him as much as is possible in this life. And desire like this is actually love, which always brings peace.[1]

There is another strategy you are welcome to try also. When you feel utterly exhausted from fighting your thoughts, say to yourself: "It is futile to contend with them any longer," and then fall down before them like a captive or coward. For in doing this you commend yourself to God in the midst of your enemies and admit the radical impotence of your nature. I advise you to remember this device particularly, for in employing it you make yourself completely supple in God's hands.[2] And surely when this attitude is authentic it is the same as self-knowledge because you have seen yourself as you really are, a miserable and defiled creature less than nothing without God. This is, indeed, experiential humility. When God beholds you standing alone in this truth he cannot refrain from hastening to you and revenging himself on your enemies. Then like a father rescuing his small child from the jaws of wild swine or savage bears, he will stoop to you and gathering you in his arms, tenderly brush away your spiritual tears.

CHAPTER 33

That through contemplation a person is purified of particular sins and their consequences, yet never arrives at perfect security in this life.

I will not go into any other techniques right now. If you master these, I believe you will be more qualified to teach me than I am to teach you. For although all I have said about their efficacy is quite true, I am far from being very skilled in them. And so I sincerely hope that you will help me by becoming proficient in them yourself.

I encourage you to keep on for this little while of time and if you cannot master these techniques immediately, endure patiently the suffering of distractions. Truly, they will be your purgatory on earth. But your suffering will pass and God will begin to teach you his own methods by grace and through

89

experience. Then I will know that you are purified of sin and its effects; from the effects of your own personal sins, that is, not from those of original sin. For the remnants of original sin will plague you to the grave despite all your efforts. They will not trouble you as much as the effects of your personal sins, however. Nevertheless, you must realize that in this life you will never be without great anguish. On account of original sin, every day will bring some new temptation to evil which you must strike down and cut away with the fierce two-edged sword of discernment. Experience will teach you that in this life there is no absolute security or lasting peace.

But never give up and do not become overly anxious about failing. For if you have the grace to conquer the effects of your personal sins with the aid of devices such as I have described (or in better ways if you can), be confident that the effects of original sin and whatever temptations may come from them will actually hinder your growth very little.

CHAPTER 34

That God gives the gift of contemplation freely and without recourse to methods; that methods alone can never induce it.

If you ask me just precisely how one is to go about doing the contemplative work of love, I am at a complete loss. All I can say is I pray that Almighty God in his great goodness and kindness will teach you himself. For in all honesty I must admit I do not know. And no wonder, for it is a divine activity and God will do it in whomever he chooses. No one can earn it. Paradoxical as it may seem, it would not even occur to a person—no, nor to an angel or saint—to desire contemplative love were it not already alive within him.[1] I believe, too, that often our Lord deliberately chooses to work in those who have been habitual sinners rather than in those who, by comparison, have never grieved him at all. Yes, he seems to do this very often. For I think he wants us to realize that he is all-merciful and almighty, and that he is perfectly free to work as he pleases, where he pleases, and when he pleases.

Yet he does not give his grace nor work this work in a person who has no aptitude for it. But a person lacking the capacity to receive his grace could never gain it through his own efforts either. No one at all, neither sinner nor innocent, can do so. For this grace is a gift, and it is not given for innocence nor *withheld* for sin. Notice I say *withheld*, not *withdrawn*. Be careful of error here, I beg you. Remember that the nearer a man comes to the truth the more sensitive he must become to error. The point I am making is correct, but if you cannot grasp it then let it be, until God himself helps you to understand. Do as I say and do not strain your mind over it.

Beware of pride; it is blasphemy against God in his gifts and it makes the sinner bold. If you were really humble you would understand what I am trying to say. Contemplative prayer is God's gift, wholly gratuitous. No one can earn it. It is in the nature of this gift that one who receives it receives also the aptitude for it. No one can have the aptitude without the gift itself. The aptitude for this work is one with the work; they are identical. He who experiences God working in the depths of his spirit has the aptitude for contemplation and no one else. For without God's grace a person would be so completely insensitive to the reality of contemplative prayer that he would be unable to desire or long for it. You possess it to the extent that you will and desire to possess it, no more and no less. But you will never desire to possess it until that which is ineffable and unknowable moves you to desire the ineffable and unknowable. Do not be curious to know more, I beg you. Only become increasingly faithful to this work until it becomes your whole life.

To put it more simply, let that mysterious grace move in your spirit as it will and follow wherever it leads you. Let it be the active doer and you the passive receiver. Do not meddle with it (as if you could possibly improve on grace), but let it be for fear you spoil it entirely. Your part is to be as wood to a carpenter or a home to a dweller. Remain blind during this time cutting away all desire to know, for knowledge is a hindrance here. Be content to feel this mysterious grace sweetly awaken in the depths of your spirit. Forget everything but God and fix on him your naked desire, your longing stripped of all self-interest.[2]

If what I speak of is your experience then be full of confidence that it really is God who, all alone, awakens your will and desire. He needs no techniques himself nor the assistance of yours. Have no fear of the evil one, for he will not dare come near you. Be he ever so cunning he is powerless to violate the inner sanctuary of your will, although he will sometimes attempt it by indirect means. Even an angel cannot touch your will directly. God alone may enter here.[3]

I am trying to make clear with words what experience teaches more convincingly, that techniques and methods are ultimately useless for awakening contemplative love. It is futile to come to this work armed with them. For all good methods and means depend on it, while it alone depends on nothing.

CHAPTER 3 5

Of Reading, Thinking, *and* Prayer, *three habits which the beginner in contemplation should develop.*

Nevertheless, anyone who aspires to contemplation ought to cultivate *Study*, *Reflection*, and *Prayer*, or to put it differently, reading, thinking, and praying. Others have written about these disciplines more comprehensively than I can here, so there is no need for me to treat of them in detail. But I will say this to those who may read this book, both beginners and those a little advanced (though not to those highly skilled in contemplation): these three are so interdependent that thinking is impossible without first reading or—what amounts to the same thing—having listened to others read. For reading and listening are really one; the priests learn from reading books and the unschooled learn from the priests who preach the word of God. Beginners and those a little advanced who do not make the effort to ponder God's word should not be surprised if they are unable to pray. Experience bears this out.

God's word, written or spoken, is like a mirror. Reason is your spiritual eye and conscience your spiritual reflection. And just as you use a mirror to detect a blemish in your physical appearance—and without a mirror or someone to tell you where the blemish is you would not discover it—so it is spiritually. Without reading or hearing God's word, a man who is spiritually blind on account of habitual sin is simply unable to see the foul stain on his conscience.

When a person discovers in a mirror—or learns from another—that his face is dirty he goes immediately to the well and washes it clean. Likewise when a man of good will sees himself as reflected by the Scriptures or the preaching of others and realizes that his conscience is defiled he also goes immediately to be cleansed. If it is a particular evil deed he notices, then the well he must seek is the Church and the water he must apply is Confession according to the custom of the Church. But if it is the blind root and tendency to sin he sees, then the well he must seek is the all-merciful God and the water he must apply is prayer with all that this implies.

So I want you to understand clearly that for beginners and those a little advanced in contemplation, reading or hearing the word of God must precede pondering it and without time given to serious reflection there will be no genuine prayer.

CHAPTER 36

Of the kind of meditations common to contemplatives.

Those, however, who are continually occupied in the work of contemplation experience all this differently. Their meditation is more like a sudden intuition or obscure certainty. For example, they will suddenly be intuitively aware of their sinfulness or God's goodness, but without having made any conscious effort to realize this through reading or other means. Insight like this is more divine than human in origin.

Actually, at this point I would not be concerned if you ceased to meditate altogether on your fallen nature or the goodness of God. I am assuming, of course, that you are drawn by grace and have asked advice about leaving these practices behind. For then it is quite sufficient to focus your attention on a simple word such as *sin* or *God* (or another one you might prefer) and without the intervention of analytical thought allow yourself to experience directly the reality it signifies. Do not use clever logic to examine or explain this word to yourself nor allow yourself to ponder its ramifications as if this sort of thing could possibly increase your love. I do not believe reasoning ever helps in the contemplative work. This is why I advise you to leave these words whole, like a lump, as it were.

When you think of sin, intend nothing in particular but only yourself, though nothing particular in yourself either. For I believe that a dark generalized awareness of sin (intending only yourself but in an undefined way, like a lump) should incite you to the fury of a caged wild animal. Anyone looking at you, however, would not notice any change in your expression, and suppose that you were quite calm and composed. Sitting, walking, lying down, resting, standing, or kneeling, you would appear completely relaxed and peaceful.

CHAPTER 37

Of the kind of personal prayers common to contemplatives.

The skilled contemplative, then, does not depend on discursive reasoning in the same way as beginners and those a little advanced in contemplation must do. His insights arise spontaneously without the help of intellectual processes, as direct intuitions of truth. Something similar may be said of his prayers, too. I am speaking now of his personal prayers, not the liturgical worship of the Church, though I do not mean to imply that liturgical prayer is neglected. On the contrary, the true contemplative has the highest esteem for the liturgy and is careful and exact in celebrating it, in continuity with the tradition of our fathers. But I am speaking now about the contemplative's personal private prayers. These, like his meditations, are wholly spontaneous and not dependent on specific methods of preparation.

Contemplatives rarely pray in words but if they do, their words are few. The fewer the better, as a matter of fact; yes, and a word of one syllable is more suited to the spiritual nature of this work than longer ones. For now the contemplative must hold himself continually poised and alert at the highest and most sovereign point of the spirit.[1]

Let me try to illustrate what I mean with an example from real life. A man or woman terrified by sudden disaster is forced by the circumstances to the limits of his personal resources, and marshals all his energy into one great cry for help. In extreme situations like this, a person is not given to many words nor even to long ones. Instead, summoning all his strength, he expresses his desperate need in one loud cry: "Help!" And with this one little word he effectively arouses the attention and assistance of others.

In a similar way, we can understand the efficacy of one little interior word, not merely spoken or thought, but surging up from the depths of a man's spirit, the expression of his whole being.[2] (By depths I mean the same as height, for in the realm of the spirit height and depth, length and breadth, are all the same.) And so this simple prayer bursting from the depths of your spirit touches the heart of Almighty God more certainly than some long psalm mumbled mindlessly under your breath. This is the meaning of that saying in Scripture: "A short prayer pierces the heavens."[3]

CHAPTER 38

How and why a short prayer pierces the heavens.

Why do you suppose that this little prayer of one syllable is powerful enough to pierce the heavens? Well, it is because it is the prayer of a man's whole being. A man who prays like this prays with all the height and depth and length and breadth of his spirit. His prayer is high, for he prays in the full power of his spirit; it is deep, for he has gathered all his understanding into this one little word; it is long, for if this feeling could endure he would go on crying out forever as he does now; it is wide, because with universal concern he desires for everyone what he desires for himself.

It is with this prayer that a person comes to understand with all the saints the length and breadth and height and depth of the eternal, gracious, almighty, and omniscient God, as St. Paul says.[1] Not completely, of course, but partially and in that obscure manner characteristic of contemplative knowledge. Length speaks of God's eternity, breadth of his love, height of his power, depth of his wisdom. Little wonder, then, that when grace so transforms a person to this image and likeness of God, his creator, his prayer is so quickly heard by God. And I feel sure that God will always hear and help a man who prays to him like this; yes, even though he be a sinner and, as it were, God's enemy. For if grace moves him to utter this anguished cry from the depths and height and length and breadth of his being, God will hear him.

Let me illustrate what I am saying with another example. Imagine that in the dead of night you heard your worst enemy cry out with his whole being "Help!" or "Fire!" Even though this man were your enemy would you not be moved to compassion by the agony of that cry and rush to help him? Yes, of course you would; and though it were in the dead of winter you would still hasten to quench the fire or calm his distress. My God! If grace can so transform a mere man to where he can forget his hatred and have such compassion for his enemy, what shall we not expect from God when he hears a person cry out to him from the height and depth and length and breadth of his whole being. For by nature God is the fullness of all that we are by participation. God's mercy belongs to the essence of his being; that is why we say he is all-merciful. Surely then we can confidently hope in him.

CHAPTER 39

How the advanced contemplative prays; what prayer is; and what words are most suited to the nature of contemplative prayer.

We must pray, then, with all the intensity of our being in its height and depth and length and breadth. And not with many words but in a little word of one syllable.

But what word shall we use? Certainly the most appro-

97

priate word is one which reflects the nature of prayer itself. And what word is that? Well, let us first try to determine the nature of prayer and then perhaps we will be in a better position to decide.

In itself, prayer is simply a reverent, conscious openness to God full of the desire to grow in goodness and overcome evil.[1] Now we know that all evil, either by instigation or deed, is summed up in the one word "sin." So when we ardently desire to pray for the destruction of evil let us say and think and mean nothing else but this little word "sin." No other words are needed. And when we intend to pray for goodness, let all our thought and desire be contained in the one small word "God." Nothing else and no other words are needed, for God is the epitome of all goodness. He is the source of all good, for it constitutes his very being.

Don't be surprised that I place these two words before all others. If I knew of any smaller words which so adequately expressed all that is good and evil, or had God taught me any others, I would certainly use them. And I advise you to do the same. Do not be anxious to investigate the nature of words or you will never get down to your task of learning to be a contemplative. For I assure you, contemplation is not the fruit of study but a gift of grace.

Even though I have recommended these two little words, you need not necessarily make them your own unless grace also inclines you to choose them. But if, through the attraction of God's grace, you do find them meaningful, then by all means fix them firmly in your mind whenever you feel drawn to pray with words because they are short and simple. If you do not feel inclined to pray with words, then forget even these.

I think you will find that the simplicity in prayer which I so highly recommend will not inhibit its frequency because, as I explained earlier, this prayer is prayed in the length of the spirit which means that it is unceasing until it is answered. Our illustration confirms this. For when a person is terrified and in great distress, he will keep crying "Help!" or "Fire!" until someone hears his plea and comes to his aid.

*That during contemplation a person leaves aside all medi-
tations on the nature of virtue and vice.*

As I have explained already, you must immerse your being
in the spiritual reality signified by the word "sin," yet without
dwelling on any particular kind of sin such as pride, anger,
envy, greed, sloth, gluttony, or lust, or on whether it is mortal
or venial sin. For to a contemplative, what does the kind or
gravity of the sin matter. In the light of contemplation anything that separates him from God, however slightly, appears
as a grievous evil and robs him of inner peace.

Let yourself experience sin as a *lump*, realizing that it is
yourself, but without defining it precisely. Then cry out in
your heart this one word "sin," "sin," "sin," or "help," "help,"
"help." God can teach you what I mean through experience
far better than I can with words. For it is best when this word
is wholly interior without a definite thought or actual sound.
Yet occasionally, you will be so satiated with the meaning of
sin that the sorrow and burden of it will flow over your body
and soul and you may burst out with the word itself.

All this is equally true of the little word "God." Immerse
yourself in the spiritual reality it speaks of yet without precise
ideas of God's works whether small or great, spiritual or
material. Do not consider any particular virtue which God
may teach you through grace, whether it is humility, charity, patience, abstinence, hope, faith, moderation, chastity,
or evangelical poverty. For to a contemplative they are, in a
sense, all the same. He finds and experiences all of them in
God, who is the source and essence of all goodness. A contemplative has come to realize that if he possesses God he
possesses all goodness and this is why he desires nothing in

particular but only the good God himself. And so you must also do, insofar as you can, with his grace. Let this little word represent to you God in all his fullness and nothing less than the fullness of God. Let nothing except God hold sway in your mind and heart.[1]

And because, as long as you are in this mortal life, you will always feel to some extent the burden of sin as part and parcel of your being, you will be wise to alternate between these two words, "God" and "sin." Keep in mind this general principle: if you possess God you will be free of sin and when you are free of sin you possess God.

CHAPTER 41

That in everything except contemplation a person ought to be moderate.

Now if you ask me what sort of moderation you should observe in the contemplative work, I will tell you: none at all. In everything else, such as eating, drinking, and sleeping, moderation is the rule. Avoid extremes of heat and cold; guard against too much and too little in reading, prayer, or social involvement. In all these things, I say again, keep to the middle path. But in love take no measure. Indeed, I wish that you had never to cease from this work of love.

But as a matter of fact, you must realize that in this life it will be impossible to continue in this work with the same intensity all the time. Sickness, afflictions of body and mind, and countless other necessities of nature will often leave you indisposed and keep you from its heights. Yet, at the same time, I counsel you to remain at it always either in earnest or, as it were, playfully. What I mean is that through desire you can remain with it even when other things intervene.

For the love of God, then, avoid illness as much as possible so that you are not responsible for unnecessary infirmity.

I am serious when I say that this work demands a relaxed, healthy, and vigorous disposition of both body and spirit. For the love of God, discipline yourself in body and spirit so that you preserve your health as long as you can. But if, despite your best efforts, illness overtakes you, be patient in bearing it and humbly wait for God's mercy. This is enough. Indeed, your patience in sickness and affliction may often be more pleasing to God than tender feelings of devotion in times of health.

CHAPTER 42

That by having no moderation in contemplation a man will arrive at perfect moderation in everything else.

Perhaps by now you are wondering how to determine the proper mean in eating, drinking, sleeping, and the rest. I will answer you briefly: be content with what comes along. If you give yourself generously to the work of love, I feel sure you will know when to begin and end every other activity. I cannot believe that a person wholeheartedly given to contemplation will err by excess or default in these external matters—unless he is a person who is always wrong.

If only I might always be preoccupied and faithful to the work of love in my heart! I doubt then that I would care much about my eating, drinking, sleeping, and speaking. For certainly it is better to achieve moderation in these things through heedlessness than through anxious introspection, as if this would help determine the appropriate measure. Surely nothing I do or say can really bring this about. Let others say what they will; experience is my witness.

So I say to you again, lift up your heart with a blind stirring of love, conscious now of sin, now of God, desiring God and detesting sin. You are only too familiar with sin, but your desire stretches out to God. I pray the good God come to your aid, for now you need him very much.

CHAPTER 43

That a man must lose the radical self-centered awareness of his own being if he will reach the heights of contemplation in this life.

Be careful to empty your mind and heart of everything except God during the time of this work. Reject the knowledge and experience of everything less than God, treading it all down beneath the *cloud of forgetting*. And now also you must learn to forget not only every creature and its deeds but yourself as well, along with whatever you may have accomplished in God's service. For a true lover not only cherishes his beloved more than himself but in a certain sense he becomes oblivious of himself on account of the one he loves.[1]

And this is what you must learn to do. You must come to loathe and regret everything that occupies your mind except God, for everything is an obstacle between you and him. It is little wonder that you should eventually hate to think about yourself in view of your deep realization of sin. This foul, wretched lump called sin is none other than yourself and though you do not consider it in detail, you understand now that it is part and parcel of your very being and something that separates you from God.

And so reject the thought and experience of all created things but most especially learn to forget yourself, for all your knowledge and experience depends upon the knowledge and feeling of yourself. All else is easily forgotten in comparison with one's own self. See if experience does not prove me

right. Long after you have successfully forgotten every creature and its works, you will find that a naked knowing and
feeling of your own being still remains between you and your
God. And believe me, you will not be perfect in love until
this, too, is destroyed.

CHAPTER 44

How a person shall dispose himself so as to destroy the
radical self-centered awareness of his being.

And now you ask me how you shall destroy this naked knowing and feeling of your own being. Perhaps you finally realize
that if you destroyed this, every other obstacle would be destroyed. If you really do understand this you have done well.
But to answer you I must explain that without God's special
grace, freely given, and without perfect correspondence to his
grace on your part, you can never hope to destroy the naked
knowing and feeling of your being. Perfect correspondence
to his grace consists in a strong, deep, interior sorrow.

But it is most important to moderate this sorrow. You must
be careful never to strain your body or spirit irreverently.
Simply sit relaxed and quiet but plunged and immersed in
sorrow. The sorrow I speak of is genuine and perfect, and
blessed is the man who experiences it. Every man has plenty
of cause for sorrow but he alone understands the deep universal reason for sorrow who experiences *that he is*. Every
other motive pales beside this one. He alone feels authentic
sorrow who realizes not only *what he is* but *that he is*. Anyone
who has not felt this should really weep, for he has never
experienced real sorrow. This sorrow purifies a man of sin and
sin's punishment. Even more, it prepares his heart to receive
that joy through which he will finally transcend the knowing
and feeling of his being.

When this sorrow is authentic it is full of reverent longing for God's salvation, for otherwise no human being could sustain it. Were he not somehow nourished by the consolation of contemplative prayer, a man would be completely crushed by the knowing and feeling of his being. For as often as he would have a true knowing and a feeling of God in purity of spirit (insofar as that is possible in this life) and then feels that he cannot—for he constantly finds his knowing and feeling as it were occupied and filled with a foul, stinking lump of himself, which must always be hated and despised and forsaken, if he shall be God's perfect disciple, taught by him alone on the mount of perfection—he almost despairs for the sorrow that he feels, weeping, lamenting, writhing, cursing, and blaming himself. In a word, he feels the burden of himself so tragically that he no longer cares about himself if only he can love God.

And yet in all this, never does he desire to not-be, for this is the devil's madness and blasphemy against God. In fact, he rejoices that he is and from the fullness of a grateful heart he gives thanks to God for the gift and the goodness of his existence. At the same time, however, he desires unceasingly to be freed from the knowing and feeling of his being.

Everyone must sooner or later realize in some manner both this sorrow and this longing to be freed. God in his wisdom will teach his spiritual friends according to the physical and moral strength of each to sustain this truth and in accordance with each one's progress and openness to his grace. He will instruct them little by little until they are completely one in the fullness of his love—that fullness possible on earth with his grace.

A good exposition of certain snares that may befall the contemplative.

I must warn you that a young novice, unseasoned by experience in contemplation, is liable to great deception unless he is constantly alert and honest enough to seek reliable guidance. The peril is that he may destroy his physical strength and fall into mental aberrations through pride, sensuality, and conceited sophistry.

This is how deception may insinuate itself. A young man or woman newly set out on the contemplative way hears about the desire in which a man lifts up his heart to God, unceasingly longing to experience his love; he also hears about the sorrow I have just described. Vainly considering himself clever and sophisticated about the spiritual life, it is not long before he begins to interpret what he hears in literal, material terms, entirely missing the deeper spiritual meaning. And so he foolishly strains his physical and emotional resources beyond reason. Neglecting the inspiration of grace and excited by vanity and conceit, he strains his endurance so morbidly that in no time he is weary and enervated in body and spirit. Then he feels the necessity to alleviate the pressure he has created by seeking some empty material or physical compensation as a relaxation for mind and body.

Should he escape this, his spiritual blindness and the abuse he inflicts on his body in this pseudo-contemplation (for it can hardly be called spiritual) may lead him to arouse his passions unnaturally or work himself into a frenzy. And all this is the result of pseudo-spirituality and maltreating the body. It is instigated by his enemy, the fiend, who takes advantage of his pride, sensuality, and intellectual conceit to deceive him.

Yet unfortunately, these people believe that the excitement they feel is the fire of love kindled in their breasts by the Holy Spirit. From this deception and the like spring evils of every kind, much hypocrisy, heresy, and error. For this sort of pseudo-experience brings with it the false knowledge of the fiend's school just as an authentic experience brings with it understanding of the truth taught by God. Believe me when I say that the devil has his contemplatives as surely as God has his.

The treachery of pseudo-experiences and false knowledge occurs in a myriad of guises and nuances according to the different mentalities and dispositions of those deceived, just as the real experience assumes many different subjective forms. But I will stop here. I do not want to burden you with more knowledge than you will need to keep you safe on your way. What will you gain from hearing how the evil one has deceived great clerics and those in different walks of life from your own? Nothing, I am sure. So I will describe only those snares you are liable to encounter as you toil at this work; I tell you so that you may be forewarned and avoid them.

CHAPTER 46

A helpful instruction on the avoidance of these snares; that in contemplation one should rely more on joyful enthusiasm than sheer brute force.

For the love of God, then, be careful and do not imprudently strain yourself in this work. Rely more on joyful enthusiasm than on sheer brute force.[1] For the more joyfully you work, the more humble and spiritual your contemplation becomes, whereas when you morbidly drive yourself, the fruits will be gross and unnatural. So be careful. Surely anyone who presumes to approach this lofty mountain of contemplative prayer through sheer brute force will be driven off with stones.[2] Stones as you know are hard, dry things that hurt terribly when they strike. Certainly morbid constraint will also hurt your health, for it is lacking the dew of grace and therefore completely dry. Besides it will do great harm to your foolish mind, leading it to flounder in diabolical illusions. So I say again, avoid all unnatural compulsion and learn to love joyfully with a sweet and gentle disposition of body and soul. Wait with gracious and modest courtesy for the Lord's initiative and do not impatiently snatch at grace like a greedy greyhound suffering from starvation.

I speak half playfully now, but try to temper the loud, crude sighing of your spirit and pretend to hide your heart's longing from the Lord. Perhaps you will scorn this as childish and frivolous but believe me, anyone who has the light to understand what I mean and the grace to follow it will experience, indeed, the delight of the Lord's playfulness. For like a father frolicking with his son, he will hug and kiss one who comes to him with a child's heart.[3]

CHAPTER 47

How one grows to the refinement of purity of spirit; how a contemplative manifests his desire to God in one way and to men in another.

Don't be put off if I seem to speak childishly and foolishly and as if I lacked sound judgment. I do so purposely, for I believe that the Lord himself has inspired me over the last few days to think and feel as I do and to tell some of my other good friends what I now tell you.

One reason I have for advising you to hide your heart's desire from God is because when you hide it I think he actually sees it more clearly. By hiding it you will actually achieve your purpose and see your desire fulfilled sooner than by any means you could devise to attract God's attention. A second reason is that I wish you to outgrow dependence on your inconstant emotions and come to experience God in the purity and depth of your spirit. And finally, I want to help you tie the spiritual knot of burning love that will bind you to God in a communion of being and desire. For as you know, God is spirit and whoever desires to be united with him must enter into the truth and depth of a spiritual communion far transcending any earthly figure.[1]

Obviously, God is all-knowing and nothing material or spiritual can actually be concealed from him, but since he is spirit, something thrust deep into the spirit is more clearly evident to him than something alloyed with emotions. And this is because the spiritual is connatural with him. For this reason I believe that to the extent that our desire is rooted in the emotions, it is more remote from God than if it awakened gently in the joyful composure of a pure, deep spirit.

Now you may understand better why I counsel you playfully to cover and conceal your desire from God. I am not suggesting that you hide it completely, for that would be the counsel of a fool and an impossible task besides. But I bid you, use your ingenuity to hide it from him as best you can. Why do I say this? Because I want you to cast it deep into your spirit far from the contagion of capricious emotions which render it less spiritual and more remote from God. Moreover, I know that as your heart grows in purity of spirit, it is less dominated by the flesh and more intimately united to God. He will see you more clearly and you will become a source of delight to him. Of course, his vision is not literally affected by this or that for it is immutable. What I am trying to convey to you is that when your heart is transformed in purity of spirit, it becomes connatural with him, for he is spirit.[2]

There is one other reason I have in advising you to conceal your longing from God. You and I and many like us are so inclined to misunderstand a spiritual reality and conceive it literally. Perhaps had I urged you to show your heart's desire to God, you would have demonstrated it physically either in gesture, sound, word, or some other strenuous activity such as you might employ to manifest a secret feeling of your heart to a human friend. But this would only render your contemplative work less simple and refined, for we show things to man in one way and to God in another.

CHAPTER 48

That God desires to be served by a man in body and soul;
that he will glorify both; and how to distinguish between
good and evil spiritual delights.

My intention in all this is certainly not to discourage you from praying out loud when the Holy Spirit inspires you to do so. And if the joy of your spirit overflows to your senses so that you begin to speak to God as you might to a man, saying such things as "Jesus," "sweet Jesus," and the like, you need not stifle your spirit. God forbid that you should misunderstand me in this matter. For truly, I do not mean to deter you from external expressions of love. God forbid that I should separate body and spirit when God has made them a unity. Indeed, we owe God the homage of our whole person, body and spirit together. And fittingly enough he will glorify our whole person, body and spirit, in eternity. In anticipation of this eternal glory, God will sometimes inflame the senses of his devout friends with unspeakable delight and consolation even here in this life. And not just once or twice but perhaps very often as he judges best. This delight, however, does not originate outside the person, entering through the windows of his faculties, but wells up from an excess of spiritual joy and true devotion of spirit.[1] Comfort and delight like this need never be doubted or feared. In a word, I believe that anyone who experiences it will not be able to doubt its authenticity.

But I advise you to be wary of other consolations, sounds, joys, or delights originating from external sources which you cannot identify, for they may be either good or evil, the work of a good angel or the work of the devil. But if you avoid vain sophistry and unnatural physical and emotional stress in the ways I have taught you (or in better ways that you may discover), it will not matter if they are good or evil, for they will be unable to harm you. Why is your security so insured? Because the source of authentic consolation is the reverent, loving desire that abides in a pure heart. This is the work of Almighty God wrought without recourse to techniques and therefore it is free of the fantasy and error liable to befall a man in this life.

As for other comforts, sounds, and delights, I will not go into the criteria for discerning whether they are good or evil just now, because I do not believe it is necessary. They are discussed thoroughly in another man's work which is far superior to anything I could write or say. You can find all I have said and all you need to know treated much better there. But what of that? I will go on anyway, for it does not weary me to reply to your heart's desire which seeks understanding of the interior life. This desire you manifested to me before in words and now I see it clearly in your actions.

One thing I will say regarding those sounds and delights which you perceive through your natural faculties and which may or may not be evil. Learn to be continually occupied in the blind, reverent, joyful longing of contemplative love as I have taught you. If you do this I am certain that this love itself will enable you to discern unerringly between good and evil. It is possible that these experiences may throw you off guard in the beginning because they are so unusual.[2] But the blind stirring of love will steady your heart and you will give them no credence until they are approved of from within by the Holy Spirit or from without by the counsel of a wise spiritual father.

CHAPTER 49

That the essence of all perfection is a good will; sensible consolations are not essential to perfection in this life.

And so you may confidently rely on this gentle stirring of love in your heart and follow wherever it leads you, for it is your sure guide in this life and will bring you to the glory of the next.[1] This little love is the essence of a good life and without it no good work is possible. Basically, love means a radical personal commitment to God. This implies that your will is harmoniously attuned to his in an abiding contentedness and enthusiasm for all he does.[2]

A good will like this is the essence of the highest perfection. The delight and consolations of sense and spirit, regardless how sublime, are but accidental to this and wholly dependent on it. I say they are accidental because it matters very little whether or not a person experiences them. They are incidental to life on earth but in eternity they will be essential elements of man's final glory, just as his body (which feels them now) will be united actually and essentially forever with his spirit. But on earth the kernel of all consolation is the inner reality of a good will. Moreover, I feel certain that a person who has matured in the perfecting of his will (at least insofar as he may in this life) experiences no earthly delight or consolation that he would not willingly and joyfully renounce if God so wished.

What is meant by pure love; that some people experience little sensible consolation while others experience a great deal.

I hope you see now why it is so important that we concentrate our whole energy and attention on this gentle stirring of love in the will. With all due reverence for God's gifts, it is my opinion that we should be quite careless of all delights and consolations of sense or spirit, regardless of how pleasurable or sublime they may be. If they come, welcome them but do not rest in them for fear of growing weak; believe me, you will expend a good deal of energy if you remain long in sweet feelings and tears. Possibly too, you may begin to love God on their account and not for himself. You will know whether or not this is happening if you become upset and irritable when you do not experience them.[1] Should you find this to be the case, then your love is not yet chaste or perfect. When love is chaste and perfect, it may allow the senses to be nourished and strengthened by sweet emotions and tears,[2] but it is never troubled if God permits them to disappear. It continues to rejoice in God all the same.

Some people experience a measure of consolation almost always while others only rarely. But God in his great wisdom determines what is best for each one. Some people are so spiritually fragile and delicate that unless they were always strengthened with a little sensible consolation, they might be unable to endure the various temptations and sufferings that afflict them as they struggle in this life against their enemies from within and without. And there are others so frail physically that they are unable to purify themselves through rigorous discipline. Our Lord in his great kindness purifies these people spiritually through consolations and tears. Yet there are others so spiritually virile that they find enough consolation in the reverent offering of this gentle, little love and in the sweet harmony of their hearts with God's. They find such spiritual nourishment within that they need little other comfort. Which of these people is holier or nearer to God, only he knows. I certainly do not.[3]

That men should be careful not to interpret literally what is meant spiritually, in particular the words "in" and "up."

And so, humbly trust the blind stirring of love in your heart. Not your physical heart, of course, but your spiritual heart, your will. Be careful that you do not interpret the spiritual things I am saying in literal terms. Believe me, the human vanity of those who have quick and imaginative minds can lead them into much error by doing just this.

Consider, for example, what I told you about hiding your desire from God as much as possible. Perhaps had I told you to show him your desire, you would have taken it more literally than you do now when I say to hide it. For now you realize that to hide something purposely is to cast it deep into your spirit. Still, I believe that great caution is necessary in interpreting words used in a spiritual sense so as not to be misled by the literal meaning. In particular, be careful of the words "in" and "up," for much error and deception in the lives of those who set out to be contemplatives can be traced to a distortion of the meaning behind these two words. I can confirm this from my own experience and from the experience of others. I think it would be useful for you to know a little about these snares.

A young disciple in God's school, who has only recently

forsaken the world, thinks that since he has given himself to prayer and penance for a short while under the guidance of his spiritual father, he is then ready to begin contemplation. He has heard others speak of it or possibly he has read about it himself. Someone like this will hear read or spoken that "a man shall draw all his faculties into himself" or that "he shall climb above himself." No sooner has he heard this when through ignorance of the interior life, sensuality, and curiosity, he completely misunderstands the meaning. He feels within himself a natural curiosity about the occult and supposes that grace is calling him to contemplation. He becomes so stubbornly attached to this conviction that should his spiritual father disagree with him, he becomes very upset. Then he begins to think and to say to others, as ignorant as himself, that no one understands him. So off he goes and, incited by boldness and presumption, leaves humble prayer and spiritual discipline too soon and begins (as he supposes) the work of contemplation. If he really persists in this, his work is neither human nor divine but, to put it bluntly, something unnatural, instigated and directed by the devil. It is a straight path to the death of body and soul, for it is an aberration leading to insanity. Yet he does not realize this and, foolishly thinking that he can possess God with his intellect, forces his mind to concentrate on nothing except God.

CHAPTER 52

How some presumptuous young beginners misinterpret "in"; the snares that result.

The breakdown I speak of comes about like this. The neophyte hears and reads that he should cease using his external faculties on external things and work interiorly. This is true as far as it goes but because he does not understand how to work interiorly, his efforts miscarry. He becomes morbidly introspective and strains his faculties, as though by brute force he could make his eyes and ears see and hear interior things. In like manner he abuses all his senses and emotions. Thus he does violence to his nature and drives his imagination so mercilessly with this stupidity that eventually his mind snaps. Then the way is clear for the evil one to feign some fantasy of light or sound, some sweet odor or delicious taste. Or the devil may excite his passions and arouse all sorts of bizarre sensations in his breast or bowels, his back, loins, and other organs.

Yet unfortunately, the poor fool is deluded by these wiles and believes that he has achieved a peaceful contemplation of God beyond all temptation to vain thoughts. Indeed, he is not altogether wrong, for he is now so satiated with lies that vain thoughts do not really trouble him. Why? Because that same fiend, who would harass him with temptations if he were engaged in genuine prayer, is the very one directing this pseudo-work and he is not so stupid as to hinder his own work with the obvious. Cleverly he leaves the fool he has trapped with lovely thoughts about God, so that his evil hand will not be detected.[1]

CHAPTER 53

Of the various inappropriate mannerisms indulged in by pseudo-contemplatives.

The spiritual and physical comportment of those involved in any sort of pseudo-contemplation is apt to appear very eccentric, whereas God's friends always bear themselves with simple grace. Anyone noticing these deluded folk at prayer might see strange things indeed! If their eyes are open, they are apt to be staring blankly like a madman or peering like one who

115

saw the devil, and well they might, for he is not far off. Sometimes their eyes look like the eyes of wounded sheep near death. Some will let their heads droop to one side, as if a worm were in their ears. Others, like ghosts, utter shrill, piping sounds that are supposed to pass for speech. They are usually hypocrites. Some whine and whimper in their desire and eagerness to be heard. This is the approach of heretics and those clever and conceited folk who argue against the truth.

Anyone observing them would undoubtedly notice many other grotesque and inappropriate mannerisms, although a few are so clever that they are able to maintain a respectable front in public. Should they be observed off guard, however, I believe their sham would be evident, and anyone with the audacity to contradict them will certainly feel their wrath. Yet they believe that all they do is for God and in the service of truth. But I am convinced that unless God intervenes with a miracle to make them renounce this specious nonsense, their way of "loving God" will drive them straight into the devil's clutches stark raving mad. I am not saying that everyone under the devil's influence is afflicted with all these affectations, though this is not impossible. But all his disciples are corrupted with some of them or with others like them, as I will explain now, God willing.

There are those so laden with all sorts of eccentric and effeminate mannerisms that when they listen they have a coy way of twisting their heads up and to one side, gaping with open mouths. One would think they were trying to hear with their mouths instead of their ears! Some, when they speak, will rudely point their fingers on their own hands or breast or at those to whom they are lecturing. Others can neither sit, stand, nor lie down without moving their feet or gesturing with their hands. Some row their arms as though they were trying to swim over a great water. Others, again, are forever grinning and giggling with every other word like giddy schoolgirls or silly clowns with no breeding. Far better a modest countenance, a calm, composed bearing, and a merry candor.

116

I am not implying that these mannerisms are greatly sinful in themselves or that all who employ them are necessarily great sinners. My point is that if these affectations dominate a person to where he is enslaved by them, they are evidence of pride, sophistry, exhibitionism, or curiosity. At the very least, they betray the fickle heart and restless imagination of one sadly lacking in a true contemplative spirit. The only reason I speak of them at all is so that the contemplative may preserve the authenticity of his own work by avoiding them.

CHAPTER 54

That contemplation graces a man with wisdom and poise and makes him attractive in body and spirit.

As a person matures in the work of love, he will discover that this love governs his demeanor befittingly both within and without. When grace draws a man to contemplation it seems to transfigure him even physically so that though he may be ill-favored by nature, he now appears changed and lovely to behold. His whole personality becomes so attractive that good people are honored and delighted to be in his company, strengthened by the sense of God he radiates.

And so, do your part to co-operate with grace and win this great gift, for truly it will teach the man who possesses it how to govern himself and all that is his. He will even be able to discern the character and temperament of others when necessary. He will know how to accommodate himself to everyone, and (to the astonishment of all) even to inveterate sinners, without sinning himself. God's grace will work through him, drawing others to desire that very contemplative love which the Spirit awakens in him. His countenance and conversation will be rich in spiritual wisdom, fire, and the fruits of love, for he will speak with a calm assurance devoid of falsehood and the fawning pretense of hypocrites.

There are some who channel all their physical and spiritual energies into learning how to support and undergird their insecurity with servile whimpering and affectations of piety. They are more anxious to *appear* holy before men than to *be* holy before God and his angels. These folk are more embarrassed and upset for a mistaken gesture or breach of etiquette in society than for a thousand vain thoughts and foul inclinations to sin, willfully encouraged or carelessly trifled with, in the presence of God and his angels. Ah, Lord God! Surely a great deal of humble affectation denotes a proud heart. It is true that a genuinely humble person ought to conduct himself with a modesty in word and manner that reflects the dispositions of his heart. But I cannot condone a halting coy voice that is contrary to the natural simplicity of one's character. If we are speaking the truth let us use a simple sincere tone of voice that accords with our personality. A person who by nature has a plain, loud voice but habitually mumbles in a craven whisper—except of course, if he is sick or is speaking in private to his Confessor or in secret to God—is plainly a hypocrite. It matters not whether he is a novice or long experienced; he is a hypocrite.

What more shall I say about these treacherous snares? Really, unless a man has the grace to quit this hypocritical whining, he is courting peril. For between the secret pride in his heart and the hypocrisy of his behavior, the poor wretch may soon drown in terrible grief.

That those who condemn sin with indiscreet zeal are deceived.

Again, the fiend will deceive some people with another insidious plot. He will fire them with a zeal to maintain God's law by uprooting sin from the hearts of others. Never will he come right out and tempt them with something obviously evil.[1] Instead, he incites them to assume the role of a zealous prelate supervising every aspect of the Christian life, like an Abbot overseeing his monks. He reprimands anyone and everyone for his faults just as if he were a legitimately constituted pastor. He feels he must rebuke them lest God's wrath descend upon himself, and he maintains that the love of God and the fire of fraternal charity impel him. But really he lies, for it is the fire of hell in his brain and imagination that incites him.[2]

The following seems to confirm this. The devil is spirit who, like the angels, has no body. But whenever by God's leave he (or any angel) assumes a body to deal with men, he will choose a body which in some way reflects the nature of his mission.[3] We see this in holy Scripture. In both the Old and New Testaments we find that when an angel was sent for any work, his body or his name reflected his spiritual message. In the same way, whenever the fiend takes human shape, some quality of his body will reflect his intention.

One particular example illustrates this very well. I have learned from some of the students of necromancy (a cult which advocates communication with the wicked spirits), and from others to whom the fiend has appeared in human guise, just what sort of body he is apt to assume. They have told me that when he appears he will usually have only one great nos-

tril, large and wide, and that he will readily toss his head
back so that a man can see straight up to his brain, which
appears like the fire of hell. A fiend can have no other brain
and he is well satisfied if he can induce a man to look at it,
for the sight will drive a human being out of his mind forever.
(The skilled apprentice of the black art is well aware of this,
however, and takes proper precautions so that he does not
endanger himself.)

So then, whenever the devil assumes a body, you may be
sure that it will in some way reflect his intention. In the case
of false zeal which we have been considering, he so inflames
the imagination of his contemplatives with the fire of hell
that suddenly and imprudently they will lash out with unbe-
lievable conceit. They arrogate to themselves the right to
admonish others, often crudely and prematurely. And all this
because they have but one spiritual nostril. The division of
a man's nose into two parts suggests that he ought to possess
a spiritual discernment enabling him to decide the good
from the bad, the bad from the worse, and the good from
the better before pronouncing judgment. (By brain I mean
the spiritual imagination, for according to nature imagination
resides and functions in the head.)

CHAPTER 56

*That those who rely more on their own natural intelligence
and human learning than on the common doctrine and
guidance of the Church are deceived.*

There are still others who, though they escape the deceptions
I have described so far, fall victim to their pride, intellectual
curiosity, and scholarly knowledge when they reject the common doctrine and guidance of the Church. These people and
their followers rely too much on their own learning. They

were never rooted in that humble, blind experience of con-templative love and the goodness of life accompanying it. Thus they are vulnerable to a pseudo-experience designed and directed by their spiritual enemy. They go so far as to rise up and blaspheme the saints, the sacraments, and the ordi-nances of Holy Church. Sensual-living men of the world who feel that the Church's requirements for the proper amend-ment of their lives are too burdensome quickly and easily follow after these heretics and fiercely support them. All this because they imagine that these heretics will lead them by a smoother path than Holy Church.

Now I really believe that anyone who will not tread the arduous way to heaven will run the easy way to hell,[1] as we shall each learn on the last day. For I am convinced that if we could see these heretics and their followers now, as clearly as we shall see them on Judgment Day, we would realize that besides their open presumption in denying the truth, they are burdened with great and terrible sins committed in their private lives. It is said of them that for all the false virtue they display in public, in private their lives are full of evil lust. In all truth they may be called the disciples of Anti-Christ.

CHAPTER 57

How some presumptuous young beginners misunderstand
the word "up"; the snares that follow.

Let us leave off this discussion now and get back to what I began to say about the spiritual understanding of certain key words.

I said earlier that young disciples of spirituality who are not wary of presumption are very inclined to misinterpret the word "up." They will hear read or spoken that contemplatives ought to "lift up their hearts to God." Right off they begin to stare up at the stars as if they were on another planet and to listen as if they hoped to catch the heavenly songs of angels. Sometimes they set their curious imagination to penetrate the secrets of the planets and to pierce the firmament in hopes of seeing into outer space. They are inclined to imagine God according to their own fancies, seeing him in sumptuous robes and setting him upon a throne in an outlandish fashion. All around him they imagine angels in human likeness arranged like musicians in an orchestra. Believe me, the like has never been seen or heard of in this life.[1]

Some of these people are unbelievably deceived by the devil, who will even send them a sort of dew which they suppose to be the heavenly food of angels. It seems to come softly and delicately out of the skies, marvelously finding its way into their mouths. Thus they are in the habit of gaping openmouthed as if they were trying to catch flies. Make no mistake. All this is an illusion despite its pious overtones, for at the same time their hearts are quite empty of genuine fervor. On the contrary, these weird fantasies have filled them with such vanity that the devil can easily go on to feign odd noises, strange illuminations, and delicious odors. It is a pitiful deceit.

Yet these folk do not see it and remain convinced that they are emulating saints like Martin, who, in a revelation, saw Christ standing among angels clad in his cloak; or Stephen, who saw the Lord standing in heaven; or the disciples, who stood watching while he was taken up into the clouds. They feel that, like them, we also should keep our gaze fixed on the heavens. Now I agree that we should lift up our eyes and hands in bodily gestures of devotion as the Spirit moves us. But I insist that our contemplative work shall not be directed up or down, to this side or that, forward or backward, as if it were a machine. For it is not a work of the flesh but an interior vital adventure pursued in the Spirit.

That certain instances in the lives of St. Martin and St.
Stephen are not to be taken as literal examples of strain-
ing upward during prayer.

Regarding what some folk say about St. Martin and St. Stephen, let us remember that although they did see visions of
Christ, these were extraordinary graces intended to confirm a
spiritual truth. These people know very well that Christ
never actually wore St. Martin's cloak—as if he had any need
of the like to protect him from the elements! No, this manifestation was for the instruction of us who are called to be
saved as members of Christ's one body. Christ was confirming
in this symbolic way what he had already taught in the Gospel. There we read that anyone who clothes the poor or minis-
ters to those in material, physical, or spiritual need for the
love of Jesus has actually ministered to Jesus himself and
will be rewarded by him. In this particular instance the Lord
in his wisdom decided to ratify the Gospel teaching with a
miracle and so he appeared to St. Martin clothed in the cloak
Martin had given to a poor man. Every revelation like this
given to men on earth has a deeper spiritual significance and
I believe that if the person receiving it could have grasped
this deeper meaning in another way the vision would have
been unnecessary.[1] So let us learn to go beyond the coarse
rind and feed on the sweet fruit.

How are we to do this? Certainly not as the heretics do,
for they are like drunkards who have drained the fair cup and
then smashed it against the wall. Let us remain in the truth
and avoid this sort of uncouth behavior. We should not so
gorge ourselves on the fruit that we become sick of the tree,
nor drink so wantonly that we smash the cup when we are

filled. Now the tree and the cup represent extraordinary visions and other felt graces such as the gestures of devotion I have spoken of. The fruit and the wine represent the deeper spiritual significance of these graces. If these gestures are inspired by the Spirit, they are meaningful and genuine; if not, they are hypocritical and false. When they are authentic they are rich in spiritual fruit and so let us not despise them. Do not noble folk reverently kiss the cup for the wine it bears?[2]

As for our Lord's physical ascension in the sight of his mother and his disciples, are contemplatives to understand this as an invitation to go stargazing during prayer, in hopes of glimpsing him enthroned in glory or standing in the heavens as St. Stephen saw him? Certainly, he does not expect us to search the heavens during the time of our spiritual work in order to behold him standing, sitting, lying down, or in any other posture for that matter. We do not really understand the nature of our Lord's glorified humanity or know what position he has assumed in heaven. This is trivia besides. What we do know is that his human body and soul are united forever with his divinity in glory. We do not know or need to know his activities, but only that he possesses himself in complete freedom. When in a vision he reveals himself in this or that posture, it is to emphasize a spiritual message and not to manifest his celestial demeanor.

Let me clarify this further with an example. Standing is symbolic of assistance or support. Before battle, for instance, one friend will say to another: "Take courage, comrade. Fight bravely and don't lose heart, for I will stand by you." Obviously he does not refer to physical posture when he says "I will stand by you," for perhaps they are moving in a cavalry troop toward a battle to be fought on horseback. He means that he will be there ready to help. Similarly, our Lord appeared standing to St. Stephen during his martyrdom to reassure him. He had no intention of giving us a lesson in daydreaming. Rather, it was as if he had said to all martyrs in the person of St. Stephen: "Look, Stephen! I have sundered the firmament to reveal myself to you standing here. Know that I am really at your side with my almighty strength ready to help you. So stand fast in your faith and bear courageously the deadly assault of those who stone you, for I will crown you with glory for your witness of me, and not only you but anyone else who suffers because he loves me."[3]

I hope you understand now that these physical revelations were intended to convey a spiritual truth, though it may be concealed from the superficial observer.

CHAPTER 59

That Christ's bodily ascension shall not be taken to prove that men should strain their minds upward during prayer; that time, place, and the body should be forgotten in contemplation.

But now you object that since our Lord ascended to his Father physically as both God and man, the ascension has both a physical and a spiritual lesson for us. To this I must reply that at his ascension our Lord's humanity had been transformed and his body, though physical, was an immortal body. He had been dead but in his resurrection he put on immortality. We know that our bodies, too, shall rise in glory on the last day. They will be spiritualized then and as mobile as our thought is now. Up or down, left or right, behind or before, will all be the same, so the theologians tell us. But we have not yet received this glory and so we can only go up to heaven in a spiritual way, which has nothing to do with direction as we commonly speak of it.

I want you to understand clearly that those who work spiritually, especially contemplatives, must be careful about the interpretation of what they read. We read "lift up" or "go in" or of a "stirring" but we must realize that these expressions are not meant in a literal, physical sense. "Stirring" does not refer to physical movement any more than "rest" refers to stationary position. For when our work is authentic and mature it is entirely spiritual, far removed from movement or repose. Besides, "stirring" could actually be better expressed as a sudden transformation than a motion. In any case, you must forget all about time, place, and matter in this spiritual work.

Be careful, then, about interpreting the ascension in gross, literal terms. Do not strain your imagination during prayer in a foolish attempt to force your body aloft as if you wanted to climb over the moon. In the sphere of the spirit all this is nonsense. As far as the physical reality of the ascension is concerned, remember that only Christ has ascended physically, as the Scriptures attest when they say, "There is no one who may ascend into heaven but only he who descended from the heavens when he became man out of love for men."[1] So that, even if it were possible for us to ascend physically now (which it is not), the cause would be an overflow of spiritual power and not the straining of our imagination up or down, to left or right. This is futile and you will be wise to avoid this error.

CHAPTER 60

That the loftiest and surest way to heaven is measured by desires and not by miles.

Perhaps Christ's ascension is still a stumbling block to you. He ascended physically in the presence of all his disciples and sent the Holy Spirit as he had promised and you feel all this proves that you should literally direct your mind upward during prayer. We do, indeed, believe that Christ in his risen humanity ascended to his Father but let me try to explain again why this should not be misconstrued in a literal sense.

I will speak as plainly as I can though my explanation may not yet be adequate.

Yes, Christ did ascend upward and from on high sent the Holy Spirit but he rose upward because this was more appropriate than to descend or to move to left or right. Beyond the superior symbolic value of rising upward, however, the direction of his movement is actually quite incidental to the spiritual reality. For in the realm of the spirit heaven is as near up as it is down, behind as before, to left or to right. The access to heaven is through desire. He who longs to be there really is there in spirit. The path to heaven is measured by desire and not by miles. For this reason St. Paul says in one of his epistles, "Although our bodies are presently on earth, our life is in heaven."[1] Other saints have said substantially the same thing but in different ways. They mean that love and desire constitute the life of the spirit. And the spirit abides where its love abides as surely as it abides in the body which it fills with life. Does this make any more sense to you? We need not strain our spirit in all directions to reach heaven, for we dwell there already through love and desire.

CHAPTER 61

That in the right order of nature the flesh is subject to the spirit and not the reverse.

All the same when at the Spirit's bidding we lift up our eyes and hands toward the heavens where the stars are fixed, we praise God with a beautiful gesture of devotion. If the Holy Spirit inspires such prayer in us, we must follow him but otherwise we should not be preoccupied with gesture because every physical gesture should be subject to the spirit and not the reverse.[1]

Our Lord's ascension bears this out. In his divinity, Jesus

had never been (nor could ever be) separated from the God-head. But when on earth the time he ordained had come for him to make his way back to the Father, he returned to his Father bodily in his Manhood. Yes, mightily and in the power of the Spirit he, as one Person, returned to the Father in his humanity. This mystery was most fittingly dramatized by his rising upward.

In a similar though less complete way, the right relationship of matter to spirit will be experienced by those who gener-ously give themselves to the interior work of love described in this book. Even though the contemplative may not con-sciously advert to it, his body will be influenced by the dispo-sition of his spirit. For when he recollects himself and begins this work, his body, which may perhaps be lounging in relax-ation, suddenly springs to attention. The inner alertness of his spirit affects the exterior disposition of his body, and how fitting that it should.

It is man's dignity to stand upright, his face toward the stars and not toward the earth like the beasts, for he is the most exalted of all God's works. The nobility of his spiritual destiny, which calls him to reach out spiritually toward God, is reflected in the bearing and dignity of his upright posture. But mark well. I said that he reaches out "spiritually" toward God, not "physically." For can a non-material spirit be di-rected hither and yon like a physical thing? By no means.

And therefore, be careful not to interpret the spiritual in material terms. It is necessary to use such words as "up," "down," "in," "out," "behind," "before," "left," and "right," for regardless how spiritual our subject, we are men and must rely on the vocabulary of ordinary human language for com-munication. Language belongs to the realm of matter because our words derive from human experience and are spoken with the physical tongue. Does this mean, however, that they must be understood in a literal sense? Of course not. As human beings we can go beyond their immediate significance to grasp the spiritual significance they bear at another level.[2]

CHAPTER 62

How a man may know when his spiritual work is beneath him, outside him, on a par with him, interior to him, and when it is above him but beneath God.

I think you would find it easier to read the spiritual meaning behind ordinary expressions if I explained certain terms commonly used in reference to the contemplative work. This may give you greater confidence in discerning accurately when you are dealing with things exterior and beneath yourself, with those interior and equal to yourself, and with those transcending yourself though still beneath God.

Beneath you and external to you lies the entire created universe. Yes, even the sun, the moon, and the stars. They are fixed above you, splendid in the firmament, yet they cannot compare to your exalted dignity as a human being.

The angels and the souls of the just are superior to you inasmuch as they are confirmed in grace and glorious with every virtue, but they are your equals in nature as intelligent creatures. By nature you are gifted with three marvelous spiritual faculties, *Mind, Reason,* and *Will,* and two secondary faculties, *Imagination* and *Feeling.* There is nothing above you in nature except God himself.

When you are reading books about the interior life and come across any references to *yourself,* understand it to mean your whole self as a human being of spiritual dignity and not merely your physical body. As man you are related to everything in creation through the medium of your faculties.

If you understand all this about the hierarchy of creation and your own nature and place in it, you will have some criteria for evaluating the importance of each of your relationships.

Of the spirit's faculties in general; how the mind as a principal power comprehends in itself all the other faculties and their works.

Reason, Will, Imagination, and Feeling are man's vital working powers through which he processes the data of reality. Mind is the comprehensive faculty which receives, sorts, and retains the knowledge acquired through the other four faculties. Since the nature of the Mind's task is so different from that of the other faculties, it is not properly said to *work* but to *understand*.

I call some of man's faculties primary and others secondary not because man's spirit is divisible but because the data they process is divisible into two main categories. The first includes all the data related to spirit, which I call primary, and the second includes everything related to matter, which I call secondary. When the two principal powers, Reason and Will, deal directly with spiritual things, they can function independently of Imagination and Feeling.

Imagination and Feeling deal with the material, both present and absent. They reside in the body and function through the medium of the body's five senses. But whereas Reason and Will function autonomously, Imagination and Feeling require the assistance of Reason and Will in order to grasp even material things in their entirety. The nature, causes, character, and excellence of material things are inaccessible to Imagination and Feeling unaided by the primary faculties.

To sum up, then, Reason and Will are called primary because they are not material and can function independently of the other faculties in the sphere of the spiritual. Imagination and Feeling are called secondary because they deal with the material and operate in the body through the medium of the five senses. Mind is a primary faculty because although it does not deal directly with the data of reality, it encompasses in itself the other four faculties, together with the knowledge they acquire. I will explain this further.

CHAPTER 64

Of the other two principal powers, Reason and Will; how they functioned before original sin.

Reason is the faculty which enables us to distinguish the bad from the good, the good from the better, and the better from the best. Or as the case may be, the good from the bad, the bad from the worse, and the worse from the worst. Before man sinned he did this naturally and easily but now Reason, blinded as a consequence of original sin, errs unless it is illumined by grace. The Mind embraces both Reason and its object.

After Reason has determined what is good, the Will moves toward it with love and desire and finally rests in it with satisfaction, delight, and full consent. Before original sin, man was in no danger of choosing and loving a false good because in his primordial integrity he experienced each thing as it really was. All his faculties were sound and he was not liable to be deceived by any of them. But in the present order of things, man cannot consistently choose the good without the assistance of grace. Original sin left him wounded and blind so that he is easily deceived by appearances and chooses an evil which has disguised itself as good.

Again, the Mind embraces both the Will and its object.

CHAPTER 65

Of the first secondary power, the Imagination; how it functions and how original sin has harmed it.

With the faculty of Imagination, we depict to ourselves the likeness of things present or absent. Imagination itself and all the images it acquires are contained in the Mind. Before original sin, Imagination co-operated completely with Reason. Like a handmaid, it faithfully reflected each image as it really was and thus Reason was never deceived in its judgments by the distorted likeness of any material or spiritual thing. Now, however, this integrity of our nature is lost, and Imagination never ceases day or night to distort the image of material creatures, to create counterfeits of their spiritual essences or to conjure up fantasies of spiritual things in our minds. Without the help of grace, it is liable to great error in perceiving and thus produces many counterfeits of reality.

The undisciplined nature of Imagination is evident in the experience of neophytes newly turned from the world and beginning to give themselves to the contemplative way of life. It is with great difficulty that they wrench their minds away from the myriad delightful thoughts, images, and day-dreams of their past which the unruly Imagination continually projects onto the screen of their minds. This habitual undisciplined activity of the Imagination is one of the painful consequences of original sin. As these neophytes progress in the practices of the contemplative life, however, meditating faithfully on their own human frailty, the Passion of Christ, his transcendent goodness, and the other truths of the interior life, Reason is gradually healed, regaining its rightful ascendancy over the Imagination.

*Of the other secondary power, Feeling; how it functions
and how original sin has harmed it.*

Feeling is the faculty of our soul which extends to the senses
and is master there. We are blessed with this faculty because
it enables us to know and experience every material creature
and to determine whether or not it is good for us. Both exterior and interior senses are included in Feeling. The exterior
senses see to the satisfaction of our physical needs and the
interior senses serve the intelligence. This is the faculty which
rebels when the body lacks any necessity and that is apt to
move us to excess in satisfying any need. It grumbles at the
deprivation of pleasure and the infliction of pain and is heart-
ily pleased when pain is removed and pleasure restored.
Again, the Mind includes in itself the faculty of Feeling and
all it experiences.

Just as Imagination is the handmaid of Reason, Feeling is
the servant of the Will. Before man sinned it was a perfect
servant, all its delight and disdain being perfectly ordered to
reality. It communicated to the Will no disordered feeling
about any material creature nor any counterfeit spiritual
experience aroused by the devil in the interior senses.

But this is no longer so. Due to original sin it experiences
pain when deprived of the inordinate pleasures it blindly
craves and when restrained by salutary discipline, which it
abhors. Grace must strengthen the Will to accept humbly
its share of original sin's consequences so that it will restrain
Feeling from overindulgence in legitimate pleasures and give
it a taste for wholesome discipline. Without grace, Feeling

would give itself up wantonly to the pleasures of life and of the flesh and so degrade a man as to render him more like a beast than a human being with a spiritual destiny.

CHAPTER 67

That ignorance of the spirit's working powers may easily lead to error in misunderstanding instruction about contemplation; how a person is made almost divine through grace.

My dear friend in God, see what liabilities we are burdened with on account of original sin. Is it any wonder that we are blind and easily deceived in understanding the spiritual meaning of certain expressions, especially if we are also ignorant of our own faculties and the way they function?

Those times that you are occupied with material things, no matter how good in themselves, you must realize that you are occupied with that which is exterior to you and beneath you in the hierarchy of nature. At other times you will be introspectively absorbed in the subtle variations of your consciousness, for as you grow in self-knowledge and human perfection, your spiritual faculties will be active in what affects your spiritual development, the good habits you acquire, the bad ones you conquer, and your relationships with others. At such times you are involved with what is interior to you and on a par with you as man. But there will come times when your mind is free of involvement with anything material or spiritual and totally taken up with the being of God himself. This is the contemplative work I have been describing in this book. And at such times you transcend yourself, becoming almost divine, though you remain beneath God.

I say you have transcended yourself, becoming almost divine, because you have gained by grace what is impossible to you by nature, for this union with God in spirit, in love, and in oneness of desire is the gift of grace. Almost divine —yes, you and God are so one that you (and any real contemplative) may in a sense truly be called divine. The Scriptures, in fact, do say this.[1] Yet, of course, you are not divine in the same way as God himself is; he without origin or end is divine by nature. You, however, were brought into being from nothingness at a certain moment in time. Moreover, after God had created you with the almighty power of his love, you made yourself less than nothing through sin. Because of sin you have not deserved anything, but the all-merciful God lovingly re-created you in grace, making you, as it were, divine and one with him for time and eternity. Yet, though you are truly one with him through grace, you remain less than him by nature.

My dear friend, do you see all I am saying? Anyone who is ignorant of his own spiritual faculties and how they function is dangerously susceptible to misunderstanding words used in a spiritual sense. Do you see more clearly now why I dared not say to you: "Show your desire to God"? Instead, I taught you to use your ingenuity and playfully conceal it. This was because I feared lest you interpret literally what I had intended spiritually.

CHAPTER 68

That nowhere spatially is everywhere spiritually; that our superficial self will ridicule contemplation as a waste of time.

Another man might tell you to withdraw all your faculties and senses within yourself and there worship God. This is well said and true besides, and no sensible person would deny it.

Yet for fear you may be deceived and interpret what I say literally, I do not choose to express the interior life in this way. Rather, I will speak in paradoxes. Do *not* try to withdraw into yourself, for to put it simply, I do not want you to be anywhere; no, not outside, above, behind, or beside yourself.

But to this you say: "Where then shall I be? By your reckoning I am to be nowhere!" Exactly. In fact, you have expressed it rather well, for I would indeed have you be nowhere. Why? Because nowhere, physically, is everywhere spiritually. Understand this clearly: your spiritual work is not located in any particular place. But when your mind consciously focuses on anything, you are there in that place spiritually, as certainly as your body is located in a definite place right now. Your senses and faculties will be frustrated for lack of something to dwell on and they will chide you for doing nothing.[1] But never mind. Go on with this nothing, moved only by your love for God. Never give up but steadfastly persevere in this nothingness, consciously longing that you may always choose to possess God through love, whom no one can possess through knowledge. For myself, I prefer to be lost in this nowhere, wrestling with this blind nothingness, than to be like some great lord traveling everywhere and enjoying the world as if he owned it.[2]

Forget that kind of everywhere and the world's all. It pales in richness beside this blessed nothingness and nowhere. Don't worry if your faculties fail to grasp it. Actually, that is the way it should be, for this nothingness is so lofty that they cannot reach it. It cannot be explained, only experienced.

Yet to those who have newly encountered it, it will feel very dark and inscrutable indeed. But truly, they are blinded by the splendor of its spiritual light rather than by any ordinary darkness.[3] Who do you suppose derides it as an emptiness? Our superficial self, of course. Certainly not our true self; no, our true, inner self appreciates it as a fullness beyond measure. For in this darkness we experience an intuitive understanding of everything material and spiritual without giving special attention to anything in particular.

CHAPTER 69

How a man's love is wonderfully transformed in the interior experience of this nothingness and nowhere.

How wonderfully is a man's love transformed by the interior experience of this nothingness and this nowhere.[1] The first time he looks upon it, the sins of his whole life rise up before him. No evil thought, word, or deed remains hidden. Mysteriously and darkly they are burned into it. No matter where he turns they confront him until after great effort, painful remorse, and many bitter tears he has largely rubbed them away.

At times the sight is as terrible as a glimpse of hell and he is tempted to despair of ever being healed and relieved of his sore burden. Many arrive at this juncture in the interior life but the terrible, comfortless agony they experience facing themselves drives them back to thoughts of worldly pleasures. They seek without for relief in things of the flesh, unable to bear the spiritual emptiness within. But they have not understood that they were not ready for the spiritual comfort which would have succored them had they waited.[2]

He who patiently abides in this darkness will be comforted and feel again a confidence about his destiny, for gradually he will see his past sins healed by grace. The pain continues yet he knows it will end for even now it grows less intense. Slowly he begins to realize that the suffering he endures is really not hell at all, but his purgatory.[3] Then will come a time when he recognizes in that nothingness no particular sin but only the lump of sin itself, which though but a form-

137

less mass is none other than himself; he sees that in himself it is the root and pain of original sin. When at other times he begins to feel a marvelous strengthening and untold delights of joy and goodness, he wonders if this nothingness is not some heavenly paradise after all. And finally there will come a moment when he experiences such peace and repose in that darkness that he thinks surely it must be God himself.

Yes, he will suppose this nothingness to be one thing and another, yet to the last it will remain a *cloud of unknowing* between him and his God.

CHAPTER 70

That as we begin to understand the spiritual where our sense-knowledge ends, so we most easily come to the highest understanding of God possible in this life with the help of grace, where our spiritual knowledge ends.

And so keep on working in this nothingness which is nowhere and do not try to involve your body's senses or their proper objects. I repeat, they are not suited to this work.[1] Your eyes are designed to see material things of size, shape, color, and position. Your ears function at the stimulation of sound waves Your nose is fashioned to distinguish between good and bad odors and your taste to distinguish sweet from sour, salt from fresh, pleasant from bitter. Your sense of touch tells you hot and cold, hard and soft, smooth and sharp.

Now, as you know, quality and quantity are not properties belonging to God or to anything spiritual. Therefore, do not try to use your interior or exterior senses to grasp the spiritual. Those who set out to work in the spirit thinking that they should see, hear, taste, smell, and feel the spiritual, either interiorly or exteriorly, are greatly deceived and violate the natural order of things. Nature designed the senses to acquire knowledge of the material world, not to understand the inner realities of the spirit. What I am trying to say is that man knows the things of the spirit more by what they are not than by what they are. When in reading or conversation we come upon things that our natural faculties cannot fathom, we may be sure that these are spiritual realities.

Our spiritual faculties, on the other hand, are equally limited in relation to the knowledge of God as he is in himself. For however much a man may know about every created spiritual thing, his intellect will never be able to comprehend the uncreated spiritual truth which is God. But there is a negative knowledge which does understand God. It proceeds by asserting everything it knows: this is not God, until finally he comes to a point where knowledge is exhausted. This is the approach of St. Denis, who said, "The most divine knowledge of God is that which is known by not-knowing."[2]

Anyone who reads Denis' book will find confirmed there all that I have been trying to teach in this book from start to finish. Except for this one statement I do not wish to quote him further, nor any other master of the interior life for that matter. There was a time when it was considered appropriately modest to say nothing of your own without substantiating it with references from Scripture or from the accepted masters, but today this sort of thing is a vain rad in conceited intellectual circles. I would rather not bother with all this since you will have no need of it anyway.

He who has ears to hear let him listen to me and he who is moved to believe me let him simply accept what I say on its own merits, for actually there is no other way.

CHAPTER 71

*That some people experience the perfection of contempla-
tion in rare moments of ecstasy called ravishing, while
others experience it as they will amid their ordinary daily
routine.*

There are some who believe that contemplation is so difficult
and so terrible an experience that no man may reach it without great struggle and then only relish it rarely in those moments of ecstasy called ravishing. Let me answer these folk
as best I can.

The truth is that God, in his wisdom, determines the
course and the character of each one's contemplative journey
according to the talents and gifts he has given him.[1] It is true
that some people do not reach contemplation without long
and arduous spiritual toil and even then only now and again
know its perfection in the delight of ecstasy called ravishing.
Yet, there are others so spiritually refined by grace and so
intimate with God in prayer that they seem to possess and
experience the perfection of this work almost as they like,
even in the midst of their ordinary daily routine, whether
sitting, standing, walking, or kneeling. They manage to retain
full control and use of their physical and spiritual faculties at
all times, however, not without some difficulty perhaps, yet
without great difficulty.

In Moses we have a type of the first kind of contemplative[2]
and in Aaron a type of the second. The Ark of the Covenant
represents the grace of contemplation and the men whose
lives were most bound up with the Ark (as the story goes)
represent those who are led by the contemplative way. Most
appropriately, too, is the Ark likened to the gift of contemplation, for as the Ark contained all the jewels and treasures

of the temple, so this little love intent upon God in the *cloud of unknowing* contains all the virtues of a man's spirit, which, as we know, is the temple of God.

Before he was permitted to gaze upon the Ark and to receive its design, Moses had to climb the long, weary path up the mountain and abide there at work in a dark cloud for six days. On the seventh day, the Lord gave him the design for the Ark's construction. In this long toil Moses endured, and in the much delayed enlightenment he finally received, we may see the pattern of those who seem to labor so long before reaching the heights of contemplation and to relish it in its fullness but seldom.

Yet what Moses gained with such great cost and enjoyed so rarely was Aaron's with seemingly little toil. For his office as priest allowed him to enter the Holy of Holies and to gaze on the Ark as often as he liked. Aaron then represents the folk I mentioned earlier who by their spiritual wisdom and the assistance of divine grace enjoy the perfect fruit of contemplation as often as they like.

CHAPTER 72

That a contemplative should not take his own experience as the criteria for other contemplatives.

It is important to realize that in the interior life we must never take our own experiences (or the lack of them) as the norm for everyone else. He who labors long in coming to contemplation and then rarely enjoys the perfection of this work may easily be deceived if he speaks, thinks, or judges other people on the basis of his own experience. In the same way, the man who frequently experiences the delight of contemplation—almost, it seems, whenever he likes—will be just as mistaken if he measures others by himself. Do not waste your time with these comparisons. For it may be that in God's wisdom those who have in the beginning struggled long and hard at prayer and only tasted its fruits occasionally may later on experience them as often as they like and in great abundance. So it was with Moses. At first he was permitted to gaze upon the Ark only now and again and not without having toiled long on the mountain, but later, when it was housed in the valley, he gazed on it as often as he liked.[1]

That the Ark of the Covenant is a figure of contemplation; that Moses, Bezaleel, and Aaron and their dealings with the Ark represent three contemplative paths.

As the Scriptures tell the story, there were three men most involved with the Ark: Moses, Bezaleel, and Aaron. On the mountain, Moses learned from God how it was to be constructed. Using the design Moses had received from God, Bezaleel fashioned it in the valley. But Aaron had care of it in the temple, seeing and touching it as often as he liked.

These three men illustrate the three ways grace may draw us to contemplation. Sometimes, like Moses, we must climb the mountain and toil with only the help of grace before reaching contemplation and then, like him, relish its fruits but rarely. (Yet in this context I want to make clear that God's self-revelation to Moses remained a gift and not the reward of his toil.) Then again, our progress in contemplation may be by way of our own spiritual insight helped by grace; then we are like Bezaleel, who could not behold the Ark until he had worked to fashion it by his own efforts, though helped by the design given to Moses on the mountain. And then there are times when grace draws us through the instrumentality of another's words. In this we are like Aaron, who was entrusted with the keeping of the Ark which Bezaleel, by the skill of his hands, fashioned and prepared.

My dear young friend, do you not see what I am trying to say? Though I have expressed it childishly and awkwardly and though I am a poor and unworthy teacher, yet I bear the office of Bezaleel in your regard, explaining and putting into your hands, as it were, this spiritual ark. But you can far surpass my crude work if you will be Aaron continually giving yourself to contemplation for both of us. I beg you to do so for the love of Almighty God. He has called us both to this work but I pray you, for the love of God, make up with your ardor what is lacking to me.

CHAPTER 74

That anyone disposed toward contemplation will recognize something akin to his own spirit when he reads this book and that only such a person should be allowed to read or hear this book; the admonitions of the Foreword are repeated.

Should it seem that the way of prayer I have described in this book is unsuited to you spiritually or temperamentally, feel perfectly free to leave it aside and with wise counsel seek another in full confidence. In that case I trust you will hold me excused for all I have written here. Truly, I wrote only according to my simple understanding of these things and with no other purpose than that of helping you. So read it over two or three times. The more often you read it the better, for that much more shall you grasp of its meaning. Parts that seemed difficult and obscure at first may perhaps become obvious and clear as you read it again.[1]

It seems to me that anyone whom grace has drawn to contemplation will not read this book (or hear it read) without feeling that it speaks of something akin to his own spirit. Should you feel this way and find it helpful, thank God with all your heart and for love of him pray for me.

I sincerely hope you will do this. But I am very serious when I ask you, for the love of God, not to share this book with anyone else unless you are convinced he is a person who will understand and appreciate it. Read again the chapter where I describe the sort of person who ought to begin the contemplative work, and you will know what sort of person I mean. And if you do share it with another, please impress upon him the importance of reading it all the way through. Without doubt there are parts which do not stand alone but require the clarification and explanation of other parts. If a person reads only the one section and not those which complement and complete it, he may easily be led into great error. So please do as I ask. And if you feel that some parts need fuller clarification, let me know which they are and what you think of them and I will revise them as best I can, according to my simple knowledge of these things.

I really do not want worldly gossips, flatterers and fault-finders, talebearers and busybodies, or the plainly curious—educated or not—to get hold of this book. I never intended to write for these folk and do not even want them to hear about it. I do not doubt that some of them may be fine people, perhaps even very fervent in the active life, but this book is not suited to their needs.[2]

CHAPTER 75

Of certain signs by which a man may determine whether or not God is drawing him to contemplation.

I would like to make clear that not everyone who reads this book (or hears it read) and finds it pleasantly interesting is therefore called to contemplation. The inner excitement he feels may not be so much the attraction of grace as the arousal of natural curiosity. But I will give you some signs for testing this inspiration so as to find its real source.[1]

In the first place, let a man examine himself to see if he has done all in his power to purify his conscience of deliberate sin according to the precepts of Holy Church and the advice of his spiritual father. If he is satisfied on this account, all is well. But to be more certain, let him see if he is habitually more attracted to this simple contemplative prayer than to any other spiritual devotion. And then, if his conscience leaves him no peace in any exterior or interior work he does unless he makes this secret little love fixed upon the *cloud of unknowing* his principal concern, it is a sign that God is calling him to this work. But if these signs are lacking, I assure you, he is not.

I am not saying that those who are being called to contemplation will feel the stirring of love continually and permanently right from the beginning, for such is not the case. In fact, the young contemplative apprentice may often completely cease to experience it for various different reasons. Sometimes God will withdraw it so that he will not begin to presume it is his own doing, or that he can control it as he likes. Presumption like this is pride. Whenever the feeling of grace is withdrawn, pride is the cause. Not necessarily because one has actually yielded to pride, but because if this grace were not withdrawn from time to time pride would surely take root. God in his mercy protects the contemplative in this way, though some foolish neophytes will think he has turned enemy to them. They fail to see how true is his friendship. At other times God may withdraw this gift when the young apprentice grows careless and begins to take it for granted. If this happens he will very likely be overwhelmed with bitter pangs of remorse. But occasionally our Lord may delay in giving it back, so that having been lost and found again it may be the more deeply appreciated.

One of the most obvious and certain signs by which a person may know if he has been called to this work is the attitude he detects in himself when he has found again the lost gift of grace. For if after long delay and inability to do this work he feels his desire for it renewed with greater passion and a deeper longing of love—so much so that (as I often think) the sorrow he felt at its loss seems like nothing at all beside his joy at finding it again—he need have no fear of error in believing that God is calling him to contemplation, regardless of what sort of person he is now or has been in the past. It is not what you are nor what you have been that God sees with his all-merciful eyes, but what you desire to be. St. Gregory declares that "all holy desires heighten in intensity with the delay of fulfillment, and desire which fades with delay was never holy desire at all." For if a man experiences less and less joy when he discovers anew the sudden presence of great desires he had formerly pursued, his first desire was not holy desire. Possibly he felt a natural tendency toward the good but this should not be confused with holy desire. St. Augustine explains what I mean by holy desire when he says that "the entire life of a good Christian is nothing less than holy desire."

My dear friend, I bid you farewell now with God's blessing and mine. May God give you and all who love him true peace, wise counsel, and his own interior joy in the fullness of grace. Amen.

THE BOOK OF
PRIVY COUNSELING

FOREWORD

My dear friend in God, this book is for you, personally, and not for the general public, for I intend to discuss your interior work of contemplation as I have come to understand it and you.[1] If I were writing for everyone, I should have to speak in general terms, but as I am writing for you alone, I will concentrate on only those things which I believe to be most personally helpful to you at this time. Should anyone else share your interior dispositions and be likely to profit from this book also, all the better. I will be delighted. But it is you alone I have in mind right now, and your interior life, as I have come to understand it. And so, to you (and others like you) I address the following pages.

CHAPTER 1

When you go apart to be alone for prayer, put from your mind everything you have been doing or plan to do. Reject all thoughts, be they good or be they evil. Do not pray with words unless you are really drawn to this; or if you do pray with words, pay no attention to whether they are many or few. Do not weigh them or their meaning. Do not be concerned about what kind of prayers you use, for it is unimportant whether or not they are official liturgical prayers, psalms hymns, or anthems; whether they are for particular or general intentions; or whether you formulate them interiorly, by thoughts, or express them aloud, in words. See that nothing remains in your conscious mind save a naked intent stretching out toward God. Leave it stripped of every particular idea *about* God (what he is like in himself or in his works) and keep only the simple awareness *that he is as he is.* Let him be thus, I pray you, and force him not to be otherwise. Search into him no further, but rest in this faith as on solid ground. This awareness, stripped of ideas and deliberately bound and anchored in faith, shall leave your thought and affection in emptiness except for a naked thought and blind feeling of your own being. It will feel as if your whole desire cried out to God and said:

> That which I am I offer to you, O Lord,
> without looking to any quality of your
> being but only to the fact that you
> are as you are; this, and nothing more.

Let that quiet darkness be your whole mind and like a mirror to you. For I want your thought of self to be as naked and as simple as your thought of God, so that you may be spiritually united to him without any fragmentation and scattering of your mind. He is your being and in him, you are what you are, not only because he is the cause and being of all that exists, but because he is *your* cause and the deep center of *your* being. Therefore, in this contemplative work think of your self and of.him in the same way: that is, with the simple awareness that he is as he is, and that you are as you are. In this way your thought will not be fragmented or scattered, but unified in him who is all.

Yet keep in mind this distinction between yourself and him: he is your being but you are not his. It is true that everything exists in him as in its source and ground of being, and that he exists in all things, as their cause and their being. Yet a radical distinction remains: he alone is his own cause and his own being. For as nothing can exist without him, so he cannot exist without himself. He is his own being and the being of everything else. Of him alone may this be said; and thus he is wholly separate and distinct from every created thing. And thus, also, he is one in all things and all things are one in him. For I repeat: all things exist in him; he is the being of all.[1]

And since this is so, let grace unite your thought and affection to him, while you strive to reject all minute inquiry into the particular qualities of your blind being or of his. Leave your thought quite naked, your affection uninvolved, and your self simply as you are, so that grace may touch and nourish you with the experimental knowledge of God as he really is. In this life, this experience will always remain dark and partial so that your longing desire for him be ever newly enkindled. Look up joyfully, then, and say to your Lord, in words or desire:

> That which I am, I offer to you,
> O Lord, for you are it entirely.

Go no further, but rest in this naked, stark, elemental awareness that you are as you are.

CHAPTER 2

It is not hard to master this way of thinking. I am certain that even the most uneducated man or woman, accustomed to a very primitive type of life, can easily learn it. Sometimes I smile to myself (though not without a touch of sadness), and marvel at those who claim that I write to you and others a complicated, difficult, lofty, and strange doctrine, intelligible to only a few clever and highly trained minds. It is not simple, uneducated folk who say this either; it is scholars and learned theologians. To these people in particular I want to reply.

It is a great pity and a sad commentary on the state of those supposedly committed to God that, in our day, not just a few people but nearly everyone (excepting one or two of God's special friends, here and there) is so blinded by a mad scramble for the latest theology or discoveries in the natural sciences that they cannot begin to understand the true nature of this simple practice; a practice so simple that even the most uneducated peasant may easily find in it a way to real union with God in the sweet simplicity of perfect love. Unfortunately, these sophisticated people are no more capable of understanding this truth in sincerity of heart than a child at his ABCs is able to understand the intricacies of erudite theologians. Yet, in their blindness, they insist on calling such a simple exercise deep and subtle; whereas, if they examined it rationally, they would discover it to be as clear and plain as the lesson of a beginner.

Surely it is beginner's fare, and I consider him hopelessly stupid and dull who cannot think and feel *that he is*; not how or what he is, but *that he is*. Such elemental self-awareness is obviously proper to the dumbest cow or most unreasonable beast. (I am being facetious, of course, for we cannot really say that one animal is dumber or more unreasonable than another.) But it is only fitting for a man to realize and experience his unique self-existence, because man stands apart in creation, far above all the beasts, as the only creature graced with reason.

And so, go down to the deepest point of your mind and think of yourself in this simple, elemental way. (Others will mean the same thing, but because of their experience, speak of the mind's "pinnacle," and of this awareness as the "highest human wisdom.") In any case, do not think *what you are* but *that you are*. For I grant that to realize what you are demands the effort of your intelligence in a good deal of thought and subtle introspection. But this you have done for quite a while with the help of God's grace; and you understand to some degree (as much as you need to for the present) just what you really are—a human being by nature and a pitiful, fallen wretch through sin. Well do you know this. Yes, and probably you feel that you know only too well, from experience, the defilements that follow and befall a man because of sin. Fie on them! Forget them, I pray you. Reflect on them no further for fear of contamination. Instead, remember that you also possess an innate ability to know *that you are*, and that you can experience this without any special natural or acquired genius.

So now, forget your misery and sinfulness and, on that simple elemental level, think only that you are as you are. I am presuming, of course, that you have been duly absolved of your sins, general and particular, as Holy Church requires. Otherwise, I should never approve of your or anyone else beginning this work. But if you think you have done your best in this matter, take up this work. You may still feel the burden of your sin and wretchedness so terribly that you are uncertain what is best for yourself, but do as I tell you now.

Take the good gracious God just as he is, as plain as a common poultice, and lay him to your sick self, just as you are.[1] Or, if I may put it another way, lift up your sick self, just as you are, and let your desire reach out to touch the good, gracious God, just as he is, for to touch him is eternal health. The woman in the Gospel testifies to this when she says: "If I but touch the hem of his garment I shall be healed."[2] She was healed physically; but even more shall you be healed of your spiritual illness by this lofty, sublime work in which your desire reaches out to touch the very being of God, beloved in himself.

Step up bravely, then, and take this medicine. Lift up your sick self, just as you are, to the gracious God, just as he is. Leave behind all inquiry and profound speculation into your being or his. Forget all these qualities and everything about them, whether they be pure or defiled, natural or grace-given, divine or human. Nothing matters now except that you willingly offer to God that blind awareness of your naked being in joyful love, so that grace can bind you and make you spiritually one with the precious being of God, simply as he is in himself.

No doubt, when you begin this practice your undisciplined faculties, finding no meat to feed upon, will angrily taunt you to abandon it. They will demand that you take up something more worthwhile, which means, of course, something more suited to them. For you are now engaged in a work so far beyond their accustomed activity that they think you are wasting your time. But their dissatisfaction, inasmuch as it arises from this, is actually a good sign, since it proves that you have gone on to something of greater value. So I am delighted. And why not? For nothing I can do, and no exercise of my physical or spiritual faculties can bring me so near to God and so far from the world, as this naked, quiet awareness of my blind being and my joyful gift of it to God.

Do not be troubled, then, if your faculties rebel and plague you to give it up. As I say, it is only because they find no meat for themselves in this practice. But you must not yield. Master them by refusing to feed them despite their rage. By feeding them, I mean giving them all sorts of intricate speculations about the details of your being to gnaw on. Meditations like this certainly have their place and value, but in comparison to the blind awareness of your being and your gift of self to God, they amount to a rupture and dispersion of that wholeness so necessary to a deep encounter with God. Therefore, keep yourself recollected and poised in the deep center of your spirit and do not wander back to working with your faculties under any pretext no matter how sublime.

Heed the counsel and instruction which Solomon gave to his son when he said:

> Worship the Lord with your substance
> and feed the poor with your first fruits.

Thus shall your barns be filled with abundance
and your presses run over with wine.[1]

Solomon said this to his son but take it as addressed to yourself, and understand it spiritually, according to the sense in
which I, standing in his place, now explain it to you.

My dear friend in God, go beyond your intellect's endless
and involved investigations and worship the Lord your God
with your whole being. Offer him your very self in simple
wholeness, all that you are and just as you are, without concentrating on any particular aspect of your being. In this way your
attention will not be scattered nor your affection entangled,
for this would spoil your singleness of heart and consequently
your union with God.

And with your first fruits feed the poor. Here he refers to
the most important of all the special gifts of nature and grace
bestowed on you at your creation and nurtured through
the years until this moment. With these God-given gifts,
these fruits, you are obliged to nourish and foster not only
yourself but also all those who are your brothers and sisters by
nature or grace. The most important of these gifts I call your
first fruits. It is the gift of being itself, the first gift each creature receives. It is true, of course, that all the attributes of
your self-existence are so intimately bound to your being as
to be actually inseparable from it. Yet, in a sense, they would
have no reality if you did not first of all exist. And therefore,
your existence deserves to be called the first of your gifts
because it really is. Your being alone shall be called your
first fruits.

If you begin to analyze thoroughly any or all of man's refined faculties and exalted qualities (for he is the noblest of
all God's creatures), you will come at length to the farthest
reaches and ultimate frontiers of thought only to find yourself
face to face with naked being itself. And if you were to use
this analysis to rouse yourself to love and praise your Lord
God who gifted you with being, and such a noble being (as
meditating on your human nature will reveal), think where it

155

would lead you. At first you might say, "I am; I see and feel that I am. And not only do I exist but I possess all sorts of personal talents and gifts." But after counting up all these in your mind, you could still go a step farther and draw them all together in a single all-embracing prayer such as this:

> That which I am and the way that I am,
> with all my gifts of nature and grace,
> you have given to me, O Lord, and you are
> all this. I offer it all to you, principally
> to praise you and to help my fellow Christians
> and myself.

Thus you can see that by pursuing your meditation to the farthest reaches and ultimate frontiers of thought, you will find yourself in the end, on the essential ground of being with the naked perception and blind awareness of your own being. And this is why your being alone can be called the first of your fruits.

So it is, that naked being takes first place among all your fruits, all the others being rooted in it. But now you have come to a time when you will no longer profit by clothing or gathering into your awareness of naked being, any or all of its particulars, by which I mean your fruits, upon which you have laboriously meditated for so long. Now it is enough to worship God perfectly with your substance, that is, with the offering of your naked being. This alone constitutes your first fruits; it will be the unending sacrifice of praise for yourself and for all men that love requires. Leave the awareness of your being unclothed of all thoughts about its attributes, and your mind quite empty of all particular details relating to your being or that of any other creature. For such thoughts will not satisfy your present need, further your growth, nor bring you and others closer to perfection. Let them alone. Truly these meditations are useless to you now. But this blind, general awareness of your being, conceived in an undivided heart, will satisfy your present need, further your growth, and bring you and all mankind closer to perfection. Believe me, it far surpasses the value of any particular thought, no matter how sublime.

CHAPTER 4

All this you can verify with the authority of the Scriptures, the example of Christ, and the scrutiny of sound logic. As all men were lost in Adam when he fell from the love which made him one with God, so all those, who, by fidelity to their own path in life, manifest their desire for salvation, will receive salvation through the Passion of Christ alone. For Christ gave himself, all that he was, as a perfect and complete sacrifice. He did not concentrate on the salvation of any one person in particular, but gave himself without reserve for all. With universal intent he made himself a true and perfect offering, giving himself without reserve so that all men might be united to his Father as effectively as he was himself.

And no greater love can any other man have than to sacrifice his very self for the good of all who are his brothers and sisters by nature or grace. For the spirit is of greater dignity than the flesh and thus it is of greater value to unite the spirit to God (who is its life) by the sublime food of love than to unite the flesh to the spirit (which is its life) by the food of earth. Of course, it is important to feed the body but unless you nourish the spirit also, you have not done everything. Both together are good, but the first, by itself, is best. For a healthy body alone will never merit salvation; but a robust spirit, even in a frail body, will not only merit salvation but reach its full perfection.

You have reached a point where your further growth in perfection demands that you do not feed your mind with meditations on the multiple aspects of your being. In the past, these pious meditations helped you to understand something of God. They fed your interior affection with a sweet and delightful attraction for him and spiritual things, and filled your mind with a certain spiritual wisdom. But now it is important that you seriously concentrate on the effort to abide continually in the deep center of your spirit, offering to God that naked blind awareness of your being which I call your first fruits. If you do this, as you may with the help of God's grace, be confident that Solomon's charge to feed the poor with your first fruits will be fully accomplished also, just as he promises; and all without your interior faculties having to seek or search carefully among the attributes of your being or of God's.

I want you to understand clearly that in this work it is not necessary to inquire into minute details of God's existence any more than of your own. For there is no name, no experience, and no insight so akin to the everlastingness of God than what you can possess, perceive, and actually experience in the blind loving awareness of this word, *is*. Describe him as you will: good, fair Lord, sweet, merciful, righteous, wise, all-knowing, strong one, almighty; as knowledge, wisdom, might, strength, love, or charity, and you will find them all hidden and contained in this little word, *is*. God in his very existence is each and all of these.[1] If you spoke of him in a hundred like ways you would not go beyond or increase the significance of that one word, *is*. And if you used none of them, you would have taken nothing from it. So be as blind in the loving contemplation of God's being as you are in the naked awareness of your own. Let your faculties rest from their minute inquiry into the attributes of his being or yours.[2] Leave all this behind and worship him with your substance: all that you are, just as you are, offered to all that he is, just as he is. For your God is the glorious being of himself and you, in the naked starkness of his being.

And thus you will bind everything together, and in a wonderful way, worship God with himself because that which you are you have from him and it is he, himself.[3] Of course, you had a beginning—that moment in time when he created you from nothing—yet your *being* has been and shall always be in him, from eternity to eternity, for he is eternal. And therefore, I will continue to cry out this one thing:

> Worship God with your substance
>   and help all mankind with your first fruits.
> Then shall your barns be filled with abundance.

The promise contained in these last words is that your interior affection will be filled with an abundance of love and practical goodness arising out of your life in God, who is your ground of being and your singleness of heart.

And your presses shall run over with wine. These presses are your interior spiritual faculties. Formerly you forced and constrained them in all kinds of meditations and rational inquiry in an effort to gain some spiritual understanding of God and yourself, of his attributes and yours. But now they are filled and overflow with wine. This wine holy Scripture speaks of is accurately and mystically understood to be that spiritual wisdom distilled in the deep contemplation and high savoring of the transcendent God.[4]

And how spontaneously, joyously, and effortlessly shall all this happen through the working of grace. Busy toil of yours is no longer necessary, for in the power of this gentle, blind contemplative work, angels will bring you wisdom. Indeed, the angels' knowledge is specially directed to this service as a handmaid to her lady.[5]

CHAPTER 6

By its very nature, this practice makes one open to the high wisdom of the transcendent God, lovingly descending into the depths of a man's spirit, uniting and binding him to God in delicate, spiritual knowledge. In great praise of this joyful, exquisite activity the wise man, Solomon, bursts out and says:

> Happy the man who finds wisdom
> and who gains understanding.
> For her profit is better than silver
> and better than gold is her revenue.
> She is the first and most pure of his fruits . . .
> My son, keep counsel and advice before you;
> They will be life to your soul
> and beauty to your mouth.
> Then you may go securely in your way,
> and your foot will not stumble.
> When you sleep you shall not fear
> you shall rest and your sleep shall be sweet.
> Be not afraid of the sudden terror
> nor of the power of the wicked falling upon you
> For the Lord will be at your side
> and he will keep your foot so that you be not taken.[1]

Let me explain the hidden meaning of what he says here.

Happy, indeed, is that man who finds the wisdom which makes him whole and binds him to God. Happy is he, who by offering to God the blind awareness of his own being enriches his interior life with a loving, delicate, spiritual knowledge that far transcends all the knowledge of natural or acquired genius. Far better this wisdom and an ease in this delicate, refined interior work than the gain of gold or silver.[2] In this passage, gold and silver symbolize all the knowledge of sense and spirit. Our natural faculties acquire this gold and silver by concentrating on things beneath us, within us, or like us, in their meditations on the attributes of God's being or the being of creatures.

He then goes on to tell why this interior work is better when he says that it is the first and most pure of a man's fruits. And little wonder, when you realize that the high spiritual wisdom gained in this work freely and spontaneously bursts up from the deepest inner ground of his spirit. It is a wisdom, dark and formless, but far removed from all the fantasies of reason or imagination. Never will the straining and toil of the natural faculties be able to produce its like. For what they produce, be it ever so sublime or subtle, when compared to this wisdom, is little more than the sham emptiness of illusion. It is as distant from the truth, visible in the radiance of the spiritual sun, as the darkness of moonbeams in a winter's night is from the splendor of the sun on the clearest day of high summer.

Then Solomon continues. He advises his son to keep this law and counsel in which all the commandments and laws of the Old and New Testaments are perfectly fulfilled, with no particular effort to concentrate on any single one of them. This interior work is called a law simply because it includes in itself all the branches and fruits of the entire law. For if you examine it wisely, you will find that its vitality is rooted and grounded in the glorious gift of love which is, as the Apostle teaches, the perfection of the whole law. "The fullness of the law is love."[3]

I tell you, that if you keep this law of love and this life-giving counsel, it really will be your spirit's life, as Solomon says. Interiorly, you will know the repose of abiding in God's love. Exteriorly, your whole personality will radiate the beauty of his love, for with unfailing truth, it will inspire you with the most appropriate response in all your dealings with your fellow Christians. And on these two activities (the interior love for God and the outward expression of your love in relating to others) depend the whole law and the prophets, as the Scriptures say. Then as you become perfect in the work of love, both within and without, you will go on your way securely grounded in grace (your guide in this spiritual journey), lovingly offering your blind, naked being to the glorious being of your God. Though they are distinct by nature, grace has made them one.

CHAPTER 7

And the foot of your love shall not stumble. This means that when, with experience, this interior work becomes a spiritual habit, you will not easily be enticed or led away from it by the meddlesome queries of your natural faculties, though in the beginning it was difficult to resist them. We might express the same thing like this: "Then the foot of your love shall neither stumble nor fall on any sort of illusion arising from the insatiable seeking of your faculties."[1] And this is because, as I said before, in the contemplative work, all their inquisitive seeking is utterly rejected and forgotten lest the human liability of falsehood contaminate the naked awareness of your blind being and draw you away from the dignity of this work.

Every particular thought of creatures that enters your mind, in addition to or instead of that simple awareness of your naked being (which is your God and your desire for him), draws you back to the business of your subtle, inquisitive faculties. Then you are no longer totally present to yourself or to your God, and this amounts to the fragmentation and scattering of any deep concentration on his being and yours. And so, with the help of his grace and the light of the wisdom that comes from perseverance in this work, remain whole and recollected in the depths of your being as often as you can.

As I have already explained to you, this simple work is not a rival to your daily activities. For with your attention centered on the blind awareness of your naked being united to God's, you will go about your daily rounds, eating and drinking, sleeping and waking, going and coming, speaking and listening, lying down and rising up, standing and kneeling, running and riding, working and resting. In the midst of it all, you will be offering to God continually each day the most precious gift you can make. This work will be at the heart of everything you do, whether active or contemplative.

Moreover, Solomon also says in this passage that if you sleep in this blind contemplation, far from all the noise and agitation of the evil one, the false world, and the frail flesh, you shall fear no peril nor any deceit of the fiend. For without doubt, when the evil one discovers you at this work, he will be utterly confused, and blinded by an agonizing ignorance of what you are doing, he will be driven by a mad curiosity to find out.[2] But never mind, *for you shall graciously take your rest* in the loving union of your spirit with God's. *Your sleep shall be untroubled*; yes, for it shall bring deep spiritual strength and nourishment to renew both your body and your spirit. Solomon confirms this shortly after when he says, *it is complete healing for the flesh.* He simply means that it will bring health to all the frailty and sickness of the flesh. And well it might, for all sickness and corruption came upon the flesh when man fell from this work. But when, with the grace of Jesus (which is always the principal agent in contemplation), the spirit again rises to it, the flesh will be completely healed. And I must remind you that it is only by the mercy of Jesus and your own loving consent that you may hope to attain this. So I add my voice to Solomon's, as he speaks in this passage, and I encourage you to stand firm in this work, continually offering God your wholehearted consent in the joy of love.

Be not afraid of the sudden terror nor of the power of the wicked . . . Here the wise man says: "Do not be overcome with anxious dread if the evil one comes (as he will) with sudden fierceness, knocking and hammering on the walls of your house; or if he should stir some of his mighty agents to rise suddenly and attack you without warning." Let us be clear about this: the fiend must be taken into account. Anyone beginning this work (I do not care who he is) is liable to feel, smell, taste, or hear some surprising effects concocted by this enemy in one or other of his senses. So do not be astonished if it happens. There is nothing he will not try in order to drag you down from the heights of such valuable work.[3] And so I tell you, watch over your heart in the day of suffering, trusting with joyful confidence in our Lord's love. For the Lord is at your side and will *keep your foot so that you be not taken.* Yes, he will be close by your side ready to help you.[4]

He will keep your foot . . . The foot he speaks of here is the love by which you mount up to God, and he promises that God will protect you so that you are not overcome by the wiles and deceits of your enemies. These, of course, are the fiend along with his cohorts, the false world and the flesh.[5]

See, my friend! Our mighty Lord, he who is love, he who is full of wisdom and power, he himself will guard, defend, and succor all who utterly forsake concern for themselves and place their love and trust in him.

CHAPTER 8

But where shall we find a person so wholeheartedly committed and firmly rooted in the faith, so sincerely gentle and true, having made self, as it were, nothing and so delightfully nourished and guided by our Lord's love? Where shall we find a loving person, rich with a transcendent experience and understanding of the Lord's omnipotence, his unfathomable wisdom and radiant goodness; one who understands so well the unity of his essential presence in all things and the oneness of all things in him[1] that he surrenders his entire being to him, in him, and by his grace, certain that unless he does he will never be perfectly gentle and sincere in his effort to make self as nothing? Where is a man of sincerity, who by his noble resolve to make self as nothing, and high desire

164

that God be all in the perfection of love, deserves to experience the mighty wisdom and goodness of God, succoring, sheltering, and guarding him from his foes within and without? Surely such a man will be deeply drenched in God's love and in the full and final loss of self as nothing or less than nothing, if less were possible; and thus he will rest untroubled by feverish activity, labor, and concern for his own wellbeing.

Keep your human objections to yourselves, you halfhearted folk! Here is a person so touched by grace that he can forsake himself in honest and unreserved selfforgetfulness. Do not tell me that by any rational appraisal he is tempting God. You say this only because you dare not do so yourselves. No, be content with your own calling in the active life; it will bring you to salvation. But leave these others alone. What they do is beyond the comprehension of your reason, so do not be shocked or surprised by their words and deeds.

Oh for shame! How long must you go on hearing or reading of all this without believing and accepting it? I refer to all our fathers wrote and spoke about in times past, to that which is the fruit and flower of the Scriptures. Either you are so blind that the light of faith can no longer help you to understand what you read, or you are so poisoned by a secret envy that you are unwilling to believe such a great good might come to your brethren and not to you. Believe me, if you are wise, you will watch out for your enemy and his insidious ways; for what he wants is to have you rely more on your own reason than on the ancient wisdom of our true fathers, the power of grace, and the designs of our Lord.

How often have you not read or heard in the holy, wise, and reliable writings of the fathers that as soon as Benjamin was born, his mother, Rachel, died. Here, Benjamin represents contemplation and Rachel represents reason. When one is touched by the grace of authentic contemplation (as he surely is in the noble resolve to make self as nothing, and the high desire that God be all), there is a sense in which we can

165

really say that reason dies. But have you not often heard and read all this in the works of various holy and scholarly men? What makes you so slow to believe it? And if you do believe it, how dare you let your prying intellect rummage among the words and deeds of Benjamin? Now Benjamin is a figure of all who have been snatched beyond their senses in an ecstasy of love,[2] and of them the prophet says: "There is Benjamin, a young child, in excess of mind."[3] I warn you: be vigilant lest you imitate those wretched human mothers who slew their newly born children. Watch, lest you accidentally thrust your bold spear with all your might at the power, wisdom, and designs of the Lord. I know you want only to further his plans; yet, if you are not careful, you may mistakenly destroy them in the blindness of your inexperience.

CHAPTER 9

In the early Church, when persecution was common, all sorts of people (not especially prepared by pious, devotional practices) were so marvelously and suddenly touched by grace that without further recourse to reason they ran to die with the martyrs. We read of craftsmen casting away their tools and of school children flinging down their books, so great was their eagerness for martyrdom. In our times the Church is left in peace, but is it so hard to believe that God still can and may touch all sorts of people with the grace of contemplative prayer in the same wonderful and unforeseen way? Is it really so strange that he should desire and actually do this? No, and I am convinced that God in his great goodness will continue to act as he wishes in those he chooses that in the end his goodness may be seen for what it is, to the astonishment of all the world. And anyone so lovingly determined to make self as nothing and so keenly desirous that God be all will most certainly be protected from the onslaught of his enemies within and without, by the gracious goodness of God himself. He need not marshal his own defenses, for with faithfulness befitting his goodness, God will unfailingly protect those who, absorbed in the business of his love, have forgotten concern for themselves. Yet, is it surprising that they are so wonderfully secure? No, for truth and gentleness have made them fearless and strong in love.

But one who does not dare abandon himself to God and criticizes others who do manifests an inner emptiness. For either the evil one has robbed his heart of the loving confidence he owes to God and the spirit of good will he owes to his fellow Christians, or else he is not yet sufficiently steeped in gentleness and truth to be a real contemplative. You, however, must not be afraid to commit yourself in radical dependence upon God or to abandon yourself to sleep in the blind contemplation of God as he is, far from the uproar of the wicked world, the deceitful fiend, and the weak flesh. Our Lord shall be at your side ready to help you; he will guard your step so that you be not taken.

It is not without reason that I liken this work to sleep. For in sleep the natural faculties cease from their work and the whole body takes its full rest, nourishing and renewing itself. Similarly, in this spiritual sleep, those restless spiritual faculties, Imagination and Reason, are securely bound and utterly emptied.[1] Happy the spirit, then, for it is freed to sleep soundly and rest quietly in loving contemplation of God simply as he is,[2] while the whole inner man is wonderfully nourished and renewed.

Do you see now why I tell you to bind up your faculties by refusing to work with them and be absorbed, instead, in offering to God the naked, blind awareness of your own being? But I say again: be sure that it is naked and not clothed in any ideas about the attributes of your being. You might be inclined to clothe it in ideas about the dignity and goodness of your being or with endless considerations of the intricate details relating to man's nature or the nature of other creatures. But as soon as you do this, you have given meat to your faculties and they will have the strength and opportunity to lead you on to all sorts of other things. I warn you, before you know it, your attention will be scattered and you will find yourself distracted and bewildered. Please be wary of this trap, I pray you.

CHAPTER 10

But perhaps your insatiable faculties have already been busy examining what I have said about the contemplative work. They are restless because it goes beyond their skill and they have left you puzzled and suspicious about this way to God. Actually, this is not surprising. For, in the past, you have been so dependent upon them that you will not easily put them aside now, even though the contemplative work requires that you do. At the moment, however, I see that your heart is troubled and wondering about all this. Is it really as pleasing to God as I say? And if so, why? I will reply to all this, but I want you to realize that these very questions arise from a mind so inquisitive that under no circumstance will it give you peace in consenting to this work, until its curiosity has been appeased to some degree by a rational explanation. But since this is the case, I will not refuse. I will yield to your proud intellect, descending to the level of your present understanding, that afterward you may rise to mine, trusting my counsel and setting no bounds to your docility. I call upon the wisdom of St. Bernard, who says that perfect docility sets no bounds.

You limit your docility when you hesitate to follow the counsel of your spiritual father before your own judgment has ratified it. See how I desire to win your confidence! Yes, I really do, and I shall. But it is love that moves me, rather than any personal ability, degree of knowledge, depth of understanding, or proficiency in contemplation itself. At any rate, I trust this is so, and pray God to supply where I fail, for my knowledge is only partial whereas his is complete.

Now to satisfy your proud intellect I will sing the praises of this work. Believe me, if a contemplative had the tongue and the language to express what he experiences, all the scholars in Christendom would be struck dumb before his wisdom. Yes, for by comparison the entire compendium of human knowledge would appear as sheer ignorance.[1] Do not be surprised, then, if my awkward, human tongue fails to explain its value adequately. And God forbid that the experience itself become so degenerate as to fit into the narrow confines of human language. No, it is not possible and certainly will never happen; and God forbid that I should ever want that! Whatever we may say of it is not it, but only about it.[2] Yet since we cannot say what it is, let us try to describe it, to the confusion of all proud intellects, especially yours, which is the actual reason for my writing at this time.

Let me begin by asking you a question. Tell me, what is the substance of man's ultimate, human perfection and what are the fruits of this perfection? I will answer for you. Man's highest perfection is union with God in consummate love, a destiny so high, so pure in itself, and so far beyond human thought that it cannot be known or imagined as it really is. Yet wherever we find its fruits, we may safely assume that it abounds. Therefore, in declaring the dignity of the contemplative work above all others, we must first distinguish the fruits of man's ultimate perfection.

These fruits are the virtues which ought to abound in every perfect man. Now, if you study carefully the nature of the contemplative work and then consider the essence and manifestation of each separate virtue, you will discover that all the virtues are clearly and completely contained in contemplation itself, unspoiled by twisted or selfish intent.[3]

I will mention no particular virtue here for it is not necessary and besides, you have read about them in my other books. It will suffice to say that the contemplative work, when it is authentic, is that reverent love, that ripe, harvested fruit of a man's heart which I told you about in my little *Letter on Prayer*. It is the *cloud of unknowing*, the secret love planted deep in an undivided heart, the Ark of the Covenant. It is Denis' mystical theology,[4] what he calls his wisdom and his treasure, his luminous darkness, and his unknown knowing. It is what leads you to a silence beyond thought and words[5] and what makes your prayer simple and brief. And it is what teaches you to forsake and repudiate all that is false in the world.

But even more, it is what teaches you to forsake and repudiate your very self according to the Gospel's demand: "Let anyone who wishes to come after me deny himself, carry his cross and follow me."[6] In the context of all we have been saying about contemplation, it is as if Christ were to say: "He who wishes to come humbly after me—not with me, but after me—to the joy of eternity or the mount of perfection . . ." Christ went ahead of us because this was his destiny by nature; we come after him by grace. His divine nature ranks higher in dignity than grace, and grace higher than our human nature. In these words he teaches us that we may follow him to the mount of perfection as it is experienced in contemplation, only if he first calls us and leads us there by grace.

This is the absolute truth. And I want you (and others like you who may read this) to understand one thing very clearly. Although I have encouraged you to set out in the contemplative way with simplicity and boldness, nevertheless I am certain, without doubt or fear of error, that Almighty God himself, independently of all techniques, must always be the chief worker in contemplation. It is he who must always awaken this gift in you by his grace. And what you (and others like you) must do is make yourselves completely receptive, consenting and suffering his divine action in the depths of your spirit.[7] Yet the passive consent and endurance you bring to this work is really a distinctively active attitude; for by the singleness of your desire ever reaching up to your Lord, you continually open yourself to his action. All this, however, you will learn for yourself through experience and the insight of spiritual wisdom.

But since God in his goodness stirs and touches different people in different ways (some through secondary causes and others directly), who dares to say that he may not be touching you and others like you through the instrumentality of this book. I do not deserve to be his servant, yet in his mysterious designs, he may work through me if he so wishes, for he is free to do as he likes. But I suppose after all that you will not really understand all this until your own contemplative experience confirms it. So I simply say: prepare yourself to receive the Lord's gift by heeding his words and realizing their full meaning. "Anyone who wishes to come after me, let him forsake himself." And tell me, what better way can one forsake and scorn himself and the world than by refusing to turn his mind to either of them or to anything about them?

CHAPTER 12

But now I want you to understand that although in the beginning I told you to forget everything save the blind awareness of your naked being, I intended all along to lead you eventually to the point where you would forget even this, so as to experience only the being of God. It was with an eye to this ultimate experience that I said in the beginning: *God is your being.* At that time I felt it was premature to expect you to rise suddenly to a high spiritual awareness of God's being. So I let you climb toward it by degrees, teaching you first to gnaw away on the naked, blind awareness of your self until by spiritual perseverance you acquired an ease in this interior work; I knew it would prepare you to experience the sublime knowledge of God's being. And ultimately, in this work, that must be your single abiding desire: the longing to experience only God. It is true that in the beginning I told you to cover and clothe the awareness of your God with the awareness of your self, but only because you were still spiritually awkward and crude. With perseverance in this practice, I expected you to grow increasingly refined in singleness of heart until you were ready to strip, spoil, and utterly unclothe your self-awareness of everything, even the elemental awareness of your own being, so that you might be newly clothed in the gracious stark experience of God as he is in himself.[1]

For this is the way of all real love. The lover will utterly and completely despoil himself of everything, even his very self, because of the one he loves. He cannot bear to be clothed in anything save the thought of his beloved.[2] And this is not a passing fancy. No, he desires always and forever to remain unclothed in full and final self-forgetting. This is love's labor;[3] yet, only he who experiences it will really understand. This is the meaning of our Lord's words: "Anyone who wishes to love me let him forsake himself." It is as if he were to say: "A man must despoil himself of his very self if he sincerely desires to be clothed in me, for I am the full flowing garment of eternal and unending love."[4]

CHAPTER 13

And so, when in this work you become aware that you are perceiving and experiencing self and not God, be filled with sincere sorrow and long with all your heart to be entirely absorbed in the experience of God alone. Cease not to desire the loss of that pitiful knowledge and corrupted awareness of your blind being. Long to flee from self as from poison. Forget and disregard your self as ruthlessly as the Lord demands.

Yet do not misunderstand my words. I did not say that you must desire to un-be, for that is madness and blasphemy

172

against God. I said that you must desire to lose the knowledge and experience of self. This is essential if you are to experience God's love as fully as possible in this life. You must realize and experience for yourself that unless you lose self you will never reach your goal. For wherever you are, in whatever you do, or howsoever you try, that elemental sense of your own blind being will remain between you and your God. It is possible, of course, that God may intervene at times and fill you with a transient experience of himself. Yet outside these moments this naked awareness of your blind being will continually weigh you down and be as a barrier between you and your God, just as in the beginning of this work the various details of your being were like a barrier to the direct awareness of your self. It is then that you will realize how heavy and painful is the burden of self. May Jesus help you in that hour, for you will have great need of him.

All the misery in the world taken together will seem as nothing beside this, because then you will be a cross to yourself. Yet this is the way to our Lord and the real meaning of his words: "Let a man first take up his cross" (the painful cross of self) that afterward he may "follow me into glory," or, as we might say, "to the mount of perfection." But listen to his promise: "There I will let him savor the delight of my love in the unspeakable experience of my divine person." See how necessary[1] it is to bear this painful burden, the cross of self. It alone will prepare you for the transcendent experience of God as he is and for union with him in consummate love.

And now as this grace touches and calls you, may you see and appreciate more and more the surpassing worth of the contemplative work.

CHAPTER 14

Tell me now, do you still expect your faculties to help you reach contemplation? Believe me, they will not. Imaginative and speculative meditations, by themselves, will never bring you to contemplative love. Be they ever so unusual, subtle, lovely, or deep; be they of your sinful past, the Passion of Christ, the joys of our Lady, or the saints and angels in heaven; or of the qualities, subtleties, and states of your being, or God's, they are useless in contemplative prayer. For myself, I choose to have nothing except that naked, blind sense of my self which I spoke of earlier.

Notice that I said *of my self* and not *of my activities*. Many people confuse their activities with themselves, believing them to be the same. But this is not so. The doer is one thing and his deeds are another. Likewise, God, as he is in himself, is quite distinct from his works which are something else again.

But returning to my point, the simple awareness of my being is all I desire, even though it must bring with it the painful burden of self and make my heart break with weeping because I experience only self and not God. I prefer it with its pain to all the subtle or unusual thoughts and ideas man may speak of or find in books (though to your clever and sophisticated mind these may seem ever so sublime and pleasant). For this suffering will set me on fire with the loving desire to experience God as he really is.

All the same, these sweet meditations do have their place and value. A newly converted sinner just beginning to pray will find in them the surest way to the spiritual awareness of himself and God. Moreover, outside of God's special intervention, I believe it is humanly impossible for a sinner to come to peaceful repose in the spiritual experience of himself and of God until he has first exercised his imagination and reason in appreciating his own human potential, as well as the manifold works of God, and until he has learned to grieve over sin and find his joy in goodness.[1] Believe me, whoever will not journey by this path will go astray. One must remain outside contemplation, occupied in discursive meditation, even though he would prefer to enter into the contemplative repose beyond them. Many mistakenly believe that they have passed within the spiritual door when, in reality, they are still outside it. What is more, they shall remain outside until they learn to seek the door in humble love. Some find the door and enter within sooner than others, not because they possess a special admittance or unusual merit, but simply because the porter chooses to let them in.

CHAPTER 15

And oh, what a delightful place is this household of the spirit! Here the Lord himself is not only the porter but the door.[1] As God, he is the porter; as man, he is the door. And thus in the Gospel he says:

> I am the door of the sheepfold
> he that enters by me shall be saved.
> He shall go in and go out
> and find pastures.
> He that enters not through the door
> but climbs up another way
> the same is a thief and a robber.[2]

In the context of all we have been saying about contemplation, you may understand our Lord's words like this: "As God, I am the all-powerful porter and therefore, it is up to me to determine who may enter and how. But I chose instead to make a common, clear way to the sheepfold, open to everyone who wanted to come. So I clothed myself in an ordinary human nature and made myself utterly available so that no one could excuse himself from coming because he did not know the way. In my humanity, I am the door and whoever comes in by way of me shall be safe."

Those who wish to enter by the door should begin by meditating on the Passion of Christ and learn to be sorry for their personal sins, which caused that Passion. Let them reprove themselves with painful remorse and stir themselves to pity and compassion for their good master, for they have deserved to suffer but did not; while he did not, and suffered so wretchedly. And then let them lift up their hearts to receive the love and goodness of their God, who chose to descend so low as to become a mortal man. Anyone who does this enters by the door and shall be safe. Whether he goes in, contemplating the love and goodness of the Godhead, or goes out, meditating on the sufferings of his humanity, he shall find the spiritual pastures of devotion in abundance. Yes, and should he advance no further in this life, he will have plenty of devotion, and more than plenty, to nourish the health of his spirit and bring him to salvation.

Yet some will refuse to enter through this door, thinking to reach perfection by other ways. They will try to get past the door with all sorts of clever speculations, indulging their unbridled and undisciplined faculties in strange, exotic fantasies, scorning the common, open entry I spoke of before and the reliable guidance of a spiritual father as well. Such a person (and I care not who he is) is not only a night thief but a day prowler. A night thief he is, for he works in the darkness of sin. Full of presumption, he trusts his own personal insights and whims more than sound advice or the security of that common, clear path I described. A day prowler he is, for under the guise of an authentic spiritual life he secretly steals and arrogates to himself the outward signs and expressions of a true contemplative, while inwardly his life bears none of its fruits. Occasionally, too, this young man may feel a slight inclination toward union with God, and blinded by this take it as approval of what he does. In reality, by yielding to his unruly desires and refusing counsel, he is on the most perilous course possible. Even greater his peril, when he is full of ambition for things high above himself and well outside the ordinary, clear path of the Christian life. This path I have already explained in the light of Christ's words, when I showed you the place and necessity of meditation. I called it the door of devotion, and I assure you it is the safest entry to contemplation in this life.

CHAPTER 16

But let us return to our subject, to what concerns you personally and those others who may share your dispositions.

Tell me now, if Christ is the door, what should a man do once he has found it? Should he stand there waiting and not go in? Answering in your place, I say: yes, this is exactly what he should do. He does well to go on standing at the door, for up till now he has lived a crude sort of existence according to the flesh, and his spirit is corroded with a great rust. It is fitting that he wait at the door until his conscience and his spiritual father agree that this rust has been largely rubbed away. But most of all, he must learn to be sensitive to the Spirit guiding him secretly in the depths of his heart and wait until the Spirit himself stirs and beckons him within. This secret invitation from God's Spirit is the most immediate and certain sign that God is calling and drawing a person to a higher life of grace in contemplation.

For it will happen that a man reads or hears about contemplation and increasingly feels in his ordinary devotions a gently mounting desire to be more intimately united to God, even in this life, through the spiritual work he has read or heard about. Certainly, this indicates that grace is touching him, because others will hear or read of the same thing and be quite unmoved, experiencing no special desire for it in their daily devotions. These folk do well to go on standing patiently at the door, as those called to salvation but not yet to its perfection.

At this point, let me digress a moment to warn you (and anyone else who may read this) of one thing in particular. It is something that applies always, but especially here, where I make a distinction between those called to salvation and those called to its perfection. Whether you feel called to one or the other is unimportant. What is important is that you

177

attend to your own calling and do not discuss or judge God's designs in the lives of others. Do not meddle in his affairs: whom he stirs and calls and whom he does not; when he calls, whether early or late; or why he calls one and not another. Believe me, if you begin judging this and that about other people you will fall into error. Pay attention to what I say and try to grasp its importance. If he calls you, praise him and pray that you may perfectly respond to his grace. If he has not called you as yet, humbly pray that he will, when the time is right. But do not presume to tell him what to do. Let him alone. He is powerful, wise, and full of desire to do the best for you and for all who love him.

Be at peace in your own calling. Whether you wait outside in meditation or come within by contemplation, you have no cause to complain; both are precious. The first is good and necessary for everyone, though the second is better. Lay hold of it, then, if you can; or rather I should say, if grace lays hold of you and if you hear our Lord's call. Yes, I speak more truly when I say this. For left to ourselves, we may proudly strain after contemplation, only to stumble in the end. Moreover, without him, it is all so much wasted effort. Remember, he himself says: "Without me you can do nothing." It is as if he were to say: "Unless I first stir you and attract you, and you then respond by consenting and suffering my action, nothing you do will completely please me." And you know by now that the contemplative work I have been describing must, of its nature, be wholly pleasing to God.

CHAPTER 17

I make this point on purpose to refute the ignorant presumption of certain people who insist that man is the principal worker in everything, even in contemplation. Relying too much on their natural cleverness and speculative theology, they say that God is the one who passively consents, even in this work. But I want you to understand that in everything touching contemplation, the contrary is true. God alone is the chief worker here, and he will act in no one who has not laid aside all exercise of his natural intellect in clever speculation.

Nevertheless, in every other good work man acts in partnership with God, using his natural wit and knowledge to the best advantage. God is fully active here also, but in a different capacity, as it were. Here he consents to the act and assists man through secondary means: the light of Scripture, reliable counsel, and the dictates of common sense, which include the demands of one's state, age, and circumstances in life. In fact, in all ordinary activities a man must never pursue an inspiration—be it ever so pious or attractive—until he has rationally examined it in the light of these three witnesses.[1]

Certainly it is reasonable to expect a man to act responsibly. Holy Church expects this and by law and decree permits no one to become a bishop (the highest degree of the active life) until she has determined by rigorous examination that he is capable of this office.

Thus, in all ordinary activities a man's native wit and knowledge (governed by the light of Scripture, good counsel, and common sense) take responsible initiative, while God graciously consents and assists in all these matters belonging to the domain of human wisdom. But in all that touches contemplation, even the loftiest human wisdom must be rejected. For here God alone is the chief worker and he alone takes the initiative, while man consents and suffers his divine action.

This, then, is the way I understand the Gospel's words: "Without me you can do nothing." They mean one thing in all ordinary activities and quite another in contemplation. All active works (whether pleasing to God or not) are done with God, but his part is, as it were, to consent and allow them. In the contemplative work, however, the initiative belongs to him alone, and he asks only that a man consent and suffer his action.[2] So you may take this as a general principle: We can do *nothing* without him; nothing good or nothing evil; nothing active or nothing contemplative.

Before I leave this point, let me add that God is with us in sin also, not because he co-operates in our sin, for he does not, but because he permits us to sin if we so choose.[3] Yes, he leaves us so free that we may go to damnation if, in the end, we choose this over sincere repentance.

In our good actions he does more than simply permit us to act. He actually assists us; to our great merit if we advance, though to our shame if we fall back. And in what touches contemplation he takes the complete initiative, first to awaken us, and then, as a master craftsman, to work in us, leading us to the highest perfection by uniting us spiritually to himself in consummate love.

And thus when our Lord says: "Without me you can do nothing," he speaks to everyone, since everyone on earth falls into one of these three groups: sinners, actives, or contemplatives. In sinners he is actively present, permitting them to do as they will; in actives, he is present, permitting and assisting; and in contemplatives, as sole master, awakening and leading them in this divine work.[4]

Alas! I have used many words and said very little. But I wanted you to understand when to use your faculties and when not to; and to see how God acts in you when you do use them, and when you do not. I felt this was important because this knowledge might prevent you from falling into certain deceptions which could otherwise have ensnared you. And since it is written, let it stand, though it is not particularly relevant to our subject. But we shall return to that now.

CHAPTER 18

With all I have said about the two callings of grace, I sense a question rising in your mind. Perhaps you are thinking something like this: "Tell me, please, is there one sign,[1] or more, to help me test the meaning of this growing desire I feel for contemplative prayer, and this delightful enthusiasm which seizes me whenever I hear or read of it? Is God really calling me through them to a more intense life of grace such as you have described in this book, or does he give them simply as food and strength for my spirit that I may wait quietly and work on in that ordinary grace which you call the door and common entry for all Christians?"

I will answer you as best I can.

You will notice, first of all, that I have given you two kinds of evidence for discerning whether or not God is calling you spiritually to contemplation. One was interior and the other exterior. Now it is my conviction that for discerning a call to contemplation, neither one, by itself, is sufficient proof. They must occur together, both indicating the same thing, before you may rely on them without fear of error.[2]

The interior sign is that growing desire for contemplation constantly intruding in your daily devotions. And there is this much I can tell you about that desire. It is a blind longing of the spirit and yet there comes with it, and lingers after it, a kind of spiritual sight which both renews the desire and increases it.[3] (I call this desire blind, because it resembles the body's faculty of motion—as in touching or walking—which as you know does not direct itself and is, therefore, in a way, blind.) So carefully observe your daily devotions and see what is happening. If they are filled with the memory of your own sinfulness, considerations of Christ's Passion, or anything else pertaining to the ordinary Christian way of prayer I have described before, know that the spiritual insight accompanying and following upon this blind desire originates in your ordinary grace. And this is a sure sign that God is not stirring you or calling you to a more intense life of grace as yet. Rather, he is giving you this desire as food and strength to go on waiting quietly and working in your ordinary grace.

The second sign is exterior and it manifests itself as a certain joyful enthusiasm welling up within you, whenever you hear or read about contemplation. I call it exterior because it originates outside you and enters your mind through the windows of your bodily senses (your eyes and ears), when you read. As for the discernment of this sign, see if that joyful enthusiasm persists, remaining with you when you have left your reading. If it disappears immediately or soon after and does not pursue you in all else you do, know that it is not a special touch of grace. If it is not with you when you go to sleep and wake up, and if it does not go before you, constantly intruding in all you do, enkindling and capturing your desire, it is not God's call to a more intense life of grace, beyond what I call the common door and entry for all Christians. In my opinion, its very transience shows that it is simply the natural joy any Christian feels when he reads or hears about the truth and more especially a truth like this, which so profoundly and accurately speaks of God and the perfection of the human spirit.

CHAPTER 19

But when the joyful enthusiasm which seizes you as you read or hear about contemplation is really the touch of God calling you to a higher life of grace, you will notice very different effects. So abounding will it be[1] that it will follow you to bed at night and rise with you in the morning. It will pursue you through the day in everything you do, intruding into your usual daily devotions like a barrier between you and them.

Moreover it will seem to occur simultaneously with that blind desire which, in the meantime, quietly grows in intensity. The enthusiasm and the desire will seem to be part of each other; so much so, that you will think it is only one desire you feel, though you will be at a loss to say just precisely what it is that you long for.[2]

Your whole personality will be transformed, your countenance will radiate an inner beauty, and for as long as you feel

182

it nothing will sadden you. A thousand miles would you run to speak with another who you knew really felt it, and yet when you got there, find yourself speechless. Let others say what they will, your only joy would be to speak of it. Your words will be few, but so fruitful and full of fire that the little you say will hold a world of wisdom (though it may seem nonsense to those still unable to transcend the limits of reason). Your silence will be peaceful, your speech helpful, and your prayer secret in the depths of your being. Your self-esteem will be natural and unspoiled by conceit, your way with others gentle, and your laughter merry, as you take delight in everything with the joy of a child. How dearly you will love to sit apart by yourself, knowing that others, not sharing your desire and attraction, would only hinder you. Gone will be all desire to read or hear books, for your only desire will be to hear of it.

Thus the mounting desire for contemplation and the joyful enthusiasm that seizes you when you read or hear of it meet and become one. These two signs (one interior and one exterior) agree, and you may rely on them as proof that God is calling you to enter within and begin a more intense life of grace.

CHAPTER 20

You will learn that all I have written of these two signs and their wonderful effects is true. And yet, after you have experienced one, or perhaps all of them, a day will come when they disappear, leaving you, as it were, barren; or, as it will probably seem to you then, worse than barren. Gone will be your new fervor, but gone, too, your ability to meditate as you had long done before. What then? You will feel as if you had fallen somewhere between the two ways having neither, yet grappling for both.[1] And so it will be; but do not be too discouraged. Suffer it humbly and wait patiently for our Lord to do as he will.[2] For now you are on what I might call a sort of spiritual ocean, in voyage from the life of the flesh to life in the spirit.

Great storms and temptations shall doubtlessly arise during this journey, leaving you bewildered and wondering which way to turn for help,[3] for your affection will feel deprived of both your ordinary grace and your special grace. Yet I say again: fear not. Even though you think you have great reason to fear, do not panic. Instead, keep in your heart a loving trust in our Lord,[4] or at any rate, do so as best you can under the circumstances. Truly, he is not far away and perhaps at any moment he will turn to you touching you more intensely than ever in the past with a quickening of the contemplative grace.[5] Then for as long as it remains, you will think you are healed and that all is well. But when you least expect,[6] it will be gone again, and again you will feel abandoned in your ship, blown hither and yon, you know not where. Still, do not lose heart. I promise you he will return and soon. In his own time he will come. Mightily and more wonderfully than ever before he will come to your rescue and relieve your anguish. As often as he goes, he will come back. And if you will manfully suffer it all with gentle love, each coming will be more marvelous and more joyful than the last.[7] Remember, all he does, he does with wise intent; he desires that you become as spiritually supple and shaped to his will as a fine Roan glove is to your hand.

And so he will sometimes go and sometimes come, that by both his presence and his absence he may prepare, educate, and fashion you in the secret depths of your spirit for this work of his. In the absence of all enthusiasm he will have you learn the real meaning of patience. With your enthusiasm gone you will think you have lost him, too, but this is not so; it is only that he wishes to teach you patience. For make no mistake about this; God may at times withdraw sweet emotions, joyful enthusiasm, and burning desires but he never withdraws his grace from those he has chosen, except in the case of deadly sin. Of this I am certain. All the rest, emotions, enthusiasm, and desires, are not in themselves grace, only tokens of grace. And these he may often withdraw, sometimes to strengthen our patience, sometimes for other reasons, but always for our spiritual good, though we may never understand. Grace, we must remember, in itself, is so high, so pure, and so spiritual that our senses and emotions are actually incapable of experiencing it.[8] The sensible fervor they experience are the tokens of grace, not grace itself. These our Lord will withdraw from time to time to deepen and mature our patience. He does so for other reasons, also, but I will not go into them right now.[9] Instead, let us get on with our subject.

CHAPTER 21

Now although you will call the delights of sensible fervor his coming, strictly speaking, this is not so.[1] Our Lord feeds and strengthens your spirit by the excellence, frequency, and deepening of those favors sometimes accompanying grace so that you may perseveringly live in his love and service. But he works in two ways. On the one hand you learn patience in their absence and on the other you grow strong with the life-giving, loving food they provide in their coming.[2] Thus our Lord fashions you by both until you become so joyfully supple and so sweetly pliable that he can lead you at last to the spiritual perfection and union with his will, which is perfect love. Then you will be as willing and content to forego all feelings of consolation, when he judges best, as to enjoy them unceasingly.

Moreover, in this time of suffering your love becomes both chaste and perfect. It is then that you will see your God and your love, and being made spiritually one with his love, nakedly experience him at the sovereign point of your spirit.[3] Here, utterly despoiled of self and clothed in nothing but him,[4] you will experience him as he really is, stripped of all the trappings of sensible delights, though these be the sweetest and most sublime pleasures possible on earth. This experience will be blind, as it must be in this life; yet, with the purity of an undivided heart, far removed from all the illusion and error liable to mortal man,[5] you will perceive and feel that it is unmistakenly he, as he really is.

Finally, the mind which sees and experiences God as he is in his naked reality is no more separate from him than he is from his own being, which, as we know, is one in essence and nature. For just as God is one with his being because they are one in nature, so the spirit, which sees and experiences him, is one with him whom it sees and experiences, because they have become one in grace.[6]

See then! Here are the signs you asked for. If you have any experience of them, you will be able to test (partially at least) the nature and meaning of the summons and awakening of grace which you feel touching you interiorly during your spiritual devotions, and exteriorly whenever you read or hear about contemplation. As a rule, few people are so singularly touched and confirmed in the grace of contemplation as to have an immediate and authentic experience of all these tokens together, in the very beginning. Yet, if you think you have really experienced one or two of them, test yourself against the rigorous criteria of Scripture, your spiritual father, and your own conscience. If you feel they all approve as one voice, it is time to lay aside speculative reasoning and profound imaginative reflections on the subtleties of your being or God's, of your activities or his. Formerly, they fed your intellect and led you beyond a worldly, material existence to the threshold of contemplation. But imagination and reason have taught you all they can and now you must learn to be wholly given to the simple spiritual awareness of your self and God.[1]

In Christ's life we have a powerful illustration of all I have been trying to say. Had there been no higher perfection possible in this life beyond seeing and loving him in his humanity, I do not believe he would have ascended into heaven while time lasted, nor withdrawn his physical presence from his friends on earth who loved him so dearly. But a higher perfection was possible to man in this life: the purely spiritual experience of loving him in his Godhead. And for this reason he told his disciples, who were loath to give up his physical presence (just as you are loath to give up the speculative reflections of your subtle, clever faculties), that for their own good he would withdraw his physical presence from them. He said to them, "It is necessary for you that I go,"[1] meaning, "It is necessary for you that I depart physically from you." The holy doctor of the Church, St. Augustine, commenting on these words, says: "Were not the form of his humanity withdrawn from our bodily eyes, love for him in his Godhead would never cleave to our spiritual eyes." And thus I say to you, at a certain point it is necessary to give up discursive meditation and learn to taste something of that deep, spiritual experience of God's love.

Relying on God's grace to lead and guide you, you will come to this deep experience of his love by following the path I have set before you in these pages. It demands that you always and ever strive toward the naked awareness of your self, and continually offer your being to God as your most precious gift. But I remind you again: see that it is naked, lest you fall into error. Inasmuch as this awareness really is naked, you will at first find it terribly painful to rest in for any length of time because, as I have explained, your faculties will find no meat for themselves in it. But there is no harm in this; in fact, I am actually delighted. Go ahead. Let them fast awhile from their natural delight in knowing. It is well said that man naturally desires to know. Yet at the same time, it is also true that no amount of natural or acquired knowledge will bring him to taste the spiritual experience of God, for this is a pure gift of grace. And so I urge you: go after experience rather than knowledge. On account of pride, knowledge may often deceive you, but this gentle, loving affection will not deceive you. Knowledge tends to breed conceit, but love builds.[2] Knowledge is full of labor, but love, full of rest.[3]

CHAPTER 24

Yet you may say: "Rest? What can he possibly be talking about? All I feel is toil and pain, not rest. When I try to follow his advice, suffering and struggle beset me on every side. On the one hand, my faculties hound me to give up this work, and I will not; on the other, I long to lose the experience of myself and experience only God, and I cannot. Battle and pain assail me everywhere. How can he talk of rest? If this is rest, I think it is a rather odd kind of rest."

My answer is simple. You find this work painful because you are not yet accustomed to it. Were you accustomed to it, and did you realize its value, you would not willingly give it up for all the material joys and rest in the world. Yes, I know, it is painful and toilsome. Still, I call it rest because your spirit does rest in a freedom from doubt and anxiety about what it must do; and because during the actual time of prayer, it is secure in the knowledge that it will not greatly err.

And so persevere in it with humility and great desire, for it is a work that begins here on earth but will go on without end into eternity. I pray that the all-powerful Jesus may bring you and all those he has redeemed by his precious blood to this glory. Amen.

NOTES for *The Cloud of Unknowing*

All cross references to the writings of St. John of the Cross are taken from *The Collected Works of St. John of the Cross* translated by Kieran Kavanaugh, O.C.D., and Otilio Rodriguez, O.C.D. (ICS Publications, Institute of Carmelite Studies, Washington, D.C.). Editions of *Ascent of Mt. Carmel, Dark Night of the Soul,* and *Living Flame of Love* are also available in Image Books in the E. Allison Peers translation.

The key to the references is as follows: A = *The Ascent of Mt. Carmel;* N = *The Dark Night;* C = *The Spiritual Canticle;* F = *The Living Flame of Love.*

Foreword	1. A, Prologue 7, 9
Chapter 1	1. C23, 2, 3
	2. N1, 1, 1, 2
Chapter 2	1. A1, 5, 8
	2. A2, 11, 8; C1, 10; C3, 9
Chapter 3	1. C29, 2; F1, 3; F3, 39
	2. A2, 9, 4; N2, 11, 1
	3. A2, 24, 4
	4. A2, 15, 4; A3, 15, 1; F3, 46
Chapter 4	1. Atom: the smallest medieval measure of time = 15/94 of a second.
	2. A2, 8, 5; A2, 24, 4
	3. A2, 8, 4
	4. F1, 13
	5. F1, 14
	6. C38, 5
	7. F1, 21
	8. C36, 5; F3, 79; Sayings: 25
	9. C25, 5; F1, 4; F1, 8; F1, 33
	10. A2, 12, 8; N1, 10, 5, 6
	11. A2, 9, 4

Chapter 5 1. A2, 16, 10; N1, 10, 2, 4; F3, 48
Chapter 6 1. A2, 8, 5
2. A2, 9, 4; A2, 24, 4
Chapter 7 1. F3, 35
Chapter 8 1. A2, 12, 8
2. A2, 8, 6; A2, 24, 4; F3, 33
3. C22, 3, 4; C27, 6
4. N2, 14, 1
5. A2, 8, 4; A2, 12, 8
Chapter 9 1. C29, 2; F1, 3; F3, 39
2. A2, 12, 8; A2, 24, 4
3. N2, 14, 1
Chapter 12 1. F1, 21
2. In the original text virtue is defined as: "nothing other than a well ordered and measured affection plainly directed to God for himself." This definition occurs several times in Richard of St. Victor. The New Catholic Encyclopedia defines virtue as: "an habitual well established readiness and disposition of man's powers directing them to specific goodness of act" (McGraw-Hill, New York, vol. 15, p. 704).
3. N1, 12, 7, 8
Chapter 14 1. N2, 18, 4
Chapter 15 1. Matt. 5:48
Chapter 16 1. Lk. 7:47
2. C29, 2
3. C9, 5; C11, 2
4. C26, 8, 14
5. C1, 17, 18
Chapter 17 1. C1, 3; C39, 13
2. C29, 1–3; F1, 9
Chapter 18 1. A2, 14, 4; F3, 43
Chapter 21 1. Chapter 8
2. A2, 14, 4; C29, 1–3; F3, 43
Chapter 22 1. Matt. 28:1–7; John 20:11–13
2. N2, 13, 6, 7
Chapter 23 1. C29, 1–3
2. Medieval form of the proverb: God helps those who help themselves.

Chapter 24 1. A1, 11, 2; A3, 38, 3
2. C29, 11
Chapter 25 1. C23, 2, 3
2. A2, 24, 8; N1, 13, 5; C24, 7
Chapter 26 1. A2, 15, 4; A3, 15, 1; F3, 46
2. A2, 8, 6; A2, 14, 12; A2, 15, 2, 5; A2, 26, 5; N2, 5, 1;
N2, 8, 4, 5; N2, 12, 2, 5; N2, 17, 2, 4; C1, 17; C7, 9
3. A2, 26, 1
Chapter 28 1. F1, 21
2. C1, 3; C39, 13
Chapter 32 1. C24, 8
2. N2, 7, 3
Chapter 34 1. F3, 71
2. A2, 12, 8; A2, 14, 12; A2, 15, 2, 5
3. N2, 23, 2, 4, 11, 12
Chapter 37 1. F1, 9–14
2. A2, 12, 6
3. F1, 33
Chapter 38 1. Eph. 3:18
Chapter 39 1. In the original text this definition of prayer reads:
"Prayer in itself properly is naught else but a devout
intent directed unto God, for the getting of good
and the removing of evil." Contrast this with the
homey, personal approach of the sixteenth-century
mystic St. Teresa: "Mental prayer is, as I see it,
simply a friendly intercourse and frequent, solitary
conversation with him who, as we know, loves us."
Life 8
Chapter 40 1. A1, 13, 4
Chapter 43 1. A1, 4, 3; C9, 6; C26, 14
Chapter 46 1. F2, 14; F3, 65
2. Heb. 12:30; Exod. 19:30
3. C6, 6
Chapter 47 1. A2, 24, 4; C11, 12; C12, 7; C22, 3, 4; C27, 6; C31, 1;
F1, 13; F2, 32, 34; F3, 78, 79
2. C31, 1; F1, 4; F3, 8
Chapter 48 1. C40, 6; F2, 14, 22
2. A3, 2, 9–12
Chapter 49 1. A3, 2, 9–12; N2, 16, 14; N2, 17, 8
2. C27, 6

Chapter 50 1. N1, 3, 1
           2. C29, 11
           3. A2, 5, 10; N1, 14, 5; F1, 24
Chapter 52 1. C16, 2
Chapter 55 1. C16, 2
           2. N1, 2, 1, 2
           3. A2, 27, 3; A2, 29, 10
Chapter 56 1. N1, Prologue
Chapter 57 1. A3, 35, 4
Chapter 58 1. A2, 17, 4, 5; A3, 31, 8, 9
           2. A2, 17, 9; A2, 29, 11
           3. A2, 19, 12, 13
Chapter 59 1. John 3:13
Chapter 60 1. Phil. 3:20
Chapter 61 1. C40, 6
           2. A2, 19, 5, 6
Chapter 67 1. Ps. 81:6: "I said 'you are gods.'" John 10:34; A2, 5,
              7; C11, 12; C12, 7, 8; C31, 1; F1, 4; F1, 13; F2,
              32, 34; F3, 8, 9, 78
Chapter 68 1. N1, 10, 5, 6
           2. C1, 12
           3. N2, 5, 1–7; N2, 8, 2–5; N2, 16, 11; N2, 17, 2–4; C13,
              1; C14–15, 16; C39, 12; F3, 49
Chapter 69 1. N2, 9, 3; N2, 24, 3
           2. N1, 11, 1–4; N1, 12, 2; N1, 14, 4; N2, 6, 1–6; N2,
              9, 1–11; C13, 1; F1, 19–22; F2, 27
           3. N2, 12, 1
Chapter 70 1. N2, 14, 1
           2. A2, 8, 6; A3, 2, 3; A3, 5, 3; C14–15, 16; F3, 49
Chapter 71 1. A2, 5, 10; F1, 24
           2. A1, 5, 6–8
Chapter 72 1. A2, 5, 10; N1, 14, 5
Chapter 74 1. A, Prologue, 8; F, Prologue, 1
           2. A, Prologue, 9
Chapter 75 1. A2, 13; N1, 9; C9, 6

NOTES for *The Book of Privy Counseling*

All cross references to the writings of St. John of the Cross are taken from *The Collected Works of St. John of the Cross* translated by Kieran Kavanaugh, O.C.D., and Otilio Rodriguez, O.C.D. (ICS Publications, Institute of Carmelite Studies, Washington, D.C.). Editions of *Ascent of Mt. Carmel, Dark Night of the Soul,* and *Living Flame of Love* are also available in Image Books in the E. Allison Peers translation.

The key to the references is as follows: A = *The Ascent of Mt. Carmel;* N = *The Dark Night;* C = *The Spiritual Canticle;* F = *The Living Flame of Love.*

Foreword   1. A1, Prologue 9
Chapter 1   1. C14–15, 5
Chapter 2   1. C11, 2, 11, 13
            2. Matt. 9:21; Mk. 5:28
Chapter 3   1. Prov. 3:9, 10
Chapter 5   1. F3, 2
            2. A2, 4, 4
            3. C38, 3; F3, 1–3
            4. C25, 7; C26, 3
            5. Ps. 122
Chapter 6   1. Prov. 3:13–14, 21–26
            2. A1, 4, 8
            3. Rom. 13:10
Chapter 7   1. A2, 1, 2
            2. N2, 23, 4, 5
            3. F3, 64
            4. C16, 2, 6
            5. C3, 6, 9
Chapter 8   1. C14–15, 5
            2. C1, 17
            3. Ps. 67:28

　　　　　　　5. A2, 1, 2
　　　　　　　6. C12, 7, 8; C22, 7; C31, 1, 2; F2, 34; F3, 8
Chapter 22　1. A2, 12, 5; F3, 65
Chapter 23　1. John 16:7
　　　　　　　2. I Cor. 8:1
　　　　　　　3. A1, 7, 4